Witches All

The Enchanted Castle   Frontispiece of Bovet's *Pandaemonium* (1684)

This old engraving depicts the sorcerer (A) abjured by the Queen (B) and her friar (C) while twelve witches dance in a fairy ring (D) and thus free the sorcerer to ride a dragon (E) to the enchanted castle (F).

Witches All

*A treasury
from past editions of*

The Witches' Almanac

REVISED EDITION

Compiled by

ELIZABETH PEPPER

Also by Elizabeth Pepper
>   *Love Charms*
>   *Celtic Tree Magic*
>   *Moon Lore*
>   *Magic Spells and Incantations*

with John Wilcock
>   *Magical & Mystical Sites, Europe and the British Isles*
>   *A Book of Days, Wisdom Through the Seasons*
>   *The Witches' Almanac*, annually

with Barbara Stacy
>   *Magical Creatures*

with the staff of *The Witches' Almanac*
>   *Magic Charms from A to Z*

To John Oliver Wilcock

Published by:
The Witches' Almanac, Ltd.
P.O. Box 289
Tiverton, RI 02878

Library of Congress Cataloging-in-Publication Data has been applied for.
ISBN 1-881098-26-5
Printed in the United States of America

Contents

And for witches,
This is law —
Where they enter in,
From *there* must they
withdraw.

Alone

From childhood's hour I have not been
As others were — I have not seen
As others saw — I could not bring
My passions from a common spring.
From the same source I have not taken
My sorrow; I could not awaken
My heart to joy at the same tone;
And all I lov'd, I lov'd alone.
Then — in my childhood — in the dawn
Of a most stormy life — was drawn
From ev'ry depth of good and ill
The mystery which binds me still:
From the torrent, or the fountain,
From the red cliff of the mountain,
From the sun that 'round me roll'd
In its autumn tint of gold —
From the thunder and the storm,
And the clouds that took the form
(When the rest of Heaven was blue)
Of a demon in my view.

— EDGAR ALLAN POE

Peasant witches "ride the air" in this vignette illustrating Martin LeFranc's poem *Le Champion des Dames*. From a French Manuscript (1440)

1 THE WITCH AND MAGIC

The Magic Craft

Centuries of arcane lore add up to the witchcraft experience. Despite the vast storehouse of knowledge that fills the world's libraries, both public and private, much occult wisdom remains oral, secrets handed down reverently from generation to generation.

But what exactly is witchcraft? That question has been answered many times and in many ways. Nearly all definitions reflect the particular concern of the writer and the prevailing thought of the time. So a seventeenth-century churchman calls witchcraft the work of the Devil, and an historian, eager to draw a parallel, declares that witch hunts result from fear, ignorance, and superstition. An anthropologist supposes witchcraft to be a survival of a pre-Christian religious expression driven underground. A psychologist calls it evidence of a disturbed mind. A social commentator views witchcraft as chicanery. A reasonable public, unreasonably, accepts any one of these answers and often attributes contrary findings to mere coincidence or historical error.

In its simplest form, the study of witchcraft is learning to understand nature and tread its paths with confidence, as a surfer is able to step on and off a wave at will, using the energy and force of the sea while accepting its immutable direction.

The theory and practice of witchcraft is possible only to those who can truly believe, but to them it becomes an unsurpassable art in which nature is neither master nor servant but an invincible ally in whose harmony all things can be achieved.

To the skeptic nothing can be taken on faith. The subconscious mind slumbers like a dormant seed deep in the earth before the sun melts the insulating snow, nurturing the quest for maturity.

But science has had its day and failed. The reigning philosophies of the past twenty centuries, with their unceasing battle against the forces of nature, have failed to bring peace and harmony to the human soul.

Now at long last the winds of change are blowing and the old ways are being re-examined. Once again the personal quest emerges and as in ancient days, witchcraft can illuminate the darkness.

There has never been a time in human history, nor any culture within that time, that lacked an occult expression. The power or magic has weathered storms of censure, ridicule and persecution, but will doubtless continue to be born and reborn in each succeeding generation.

That the magic of witchcraft cannot be precisely defined, explained or categorized is one of its strengths. Those blessed with an occult sense, that special awareness, have no need to prove it. It is as natural as breathing. "I know mine and mine know me" might well apply to the craft, for attraction to its doctrines will appear in early childhood despite all manner of forces that may be applied to thwart it.

And as we believe in reincarnation, the transmigration of souls, a constant replenishment of our circle serves to remind us that energy cannot die but merely changes form. Poet Robert Graves and psychologist Carl Jung, while seeking other goals, may have succeeded in uncovering a glimpse of the true nature of witchcraft. Graves in *The White Goddess* suggests the presence of natural occult power in humans and equates it with poetic inspiration. Jung's theory of a collective unconscious mind through which pass racial traits, myths, and instinctive memories illuminates dream knowledge.

But these are hints and nothing more. If the occult attracts you and you are mysteriously aware of unseen forces, you may possess a faculty bestowed on some and denied to others. Accept your gift. Don't try to explain it even to yourself. Much in life is too elusive to be put into words. Indeed, many things are not as yet explainable in existing terms. Keats wrote that "*Heard melodies are sweet, but those unheard / Are sweeter; therefore, ye soft pipes, play on.*"

Turn the page. Our music begins…

Are You a Witch?

Reincarnation is a basic tenet of witchcraft. Those of us fortunate enough to belong to the craft believe that successive lives are enjoyed under the same zodiac sign. But unlike other ideologies, witchcraft imposes no demands for increasing excellence — only that each life be lived to its fullest capabilities.

Most people, despite centuries of indoctrination by a mechanized society, still have ties to the earth, some innate witchcraft potential that can be developed. See how you react to these questions:

1. Have you always been intrigued by the occult?
2. Do you prefer the night to day?
3. Does a storm stir in you an inexplicable sense of excitement?
4. Are you a sensualist?
5. Have you always felt different from most people around you?
6. Do you instinctively respond to animals?
7. Are you comfortable alone?
8. Are you relatively indifferent to material possessions?
9. Have you had fleeting glimpses of former lives?

If you find you can answer most of these questions in the affirmative, your witch potential is probably high and should be encouraged.

There is no church to join, no tribute to pay and no hierarchy to dictate. You, and you alone, must concentrate on the development of your own other-consciousness. Go to nature and observe. Attune your inner mechanism to the quiet pace of the seasons and the procession of the constellations across the sky. Go alone or with that person closest to you. Watch the moon rise, walk in the forests. Touch the earth, drink the water, breathe the air. And then light the sacred candle and begin the life you were meant to live.

Aradia's Gifts

The legend of Aradia came to light just before the turn of the twentieth century when Maddalena, an Italian witch, delivered to occultist Charles G. Leland a manuscript called the "*Vangelo della Streghe*." Leland assumed the material had been set down from oral narration of tales and traditions reaching back to Etruscan times. From this source Leland derived his book *Aradia*. Realizing that *Aradia* would find a limited audience, Leland noted in the preface, "There are few indeed who will care whether there is a veritable Gospel of Witches, apparently of extreme antiquity, embodying the belief in a strange counter-religion which has held its own from prehistoric time to the present day." And nearly seventy-five years would pass before the lore Leland regarded "as something to say the least remarkable" would begin to receive the attention and appreciation it deserves.

Illustrations by C.G. Leland (1891)

Among the conjurations, spells and invocations of the *Vangelo* we find the allegorical tale of Aradia, born of the mating between the Lady of Darkness (Diana) and the Lord of Light (Lucifer), destined to teach the secret art of witchcraft to the children of Earth. Upon those Aradia favored were bestowed certain symbolic gifts.

- *To know success in love*
- *To bless or curse with power friends and enemies*
- *To converse with spirits*
- *To find hidden treasures in ancient ruins*
- *To conjure spirits of those who died leaving treasures*
- *To understand the voice of the wind*

- *To change water into wine*
- *To divine with cards*
- *To know the secrets of the hand*
- *To cure diseases*
- *To make those who are ugly beautiful*
- *To tame wild beasts*

Witch Words

Language is a symbolic system revealing human concerns and cultural concepts. If individuals possessing what seemed to be mystical wisdom or uncanny power had never existed, a word defining them would not have evolved. Significantly nearly every culture in all of recorded time has an equivalent for the word "witch."

The Old English "wicca" (masculine) and "wicce" (feminine) took the form "wicche" in Middle English to include both genders. By the sixteenth century, wicche had become synonymous with cunning or wise man/woman, leading many semanticists to conclude that "witch" originally derived from the Anglo-Saxon "wita" meaning wise. A random sampling of the word in other languages:

BULGARIAN — *viestae* (m.)
    vjescirica (f.)
CAMBODIAN — *àp thmòp* (m.)
    mi thmòp (f.)
DALMATIAN — *macisnica* or
    krstaca
DANISH — *heks*
DUTCH — *hexe*
ESKIMO — *angakok*
FRENCH — *sorcier* (m.)
    sorcière (f.)
GERMAN — *die hexe* or
    wickhersen
GREEK — *mágissa*

HAWAIIAN — *wahine kilokilo*
HINDUSTANI — *jádúgarní*
ICELANDIC — *vitka*
IRISH — *badb* or *bov*
ITALIAN — *stregone* (m.)
    strega (f.)
JAPANESE — *ichiko* or *miko*
LATIN — *magus* (m.)
    saga (f.)
NAVAHO — *adant'i*
NORWEGIAN — *trollmann* (m.)
    trollkjerring (f.)
    heks
POLISH — *czarowniea*

PORTUGUESE — *feiticeiro* (m.)
    feiticeria (f.)
RUSSIAN — *koldoon* (m.)
    koldoonia (f.)
ROMANY — *chov-hani* or
    chorihani
SERBIAN — *vjestica*
SPANISH — *brujo* (m.)
    bruja (f.)
SWEDISH — *trollkarl* (m.)
    trollkvinna (f.)
    häxa
TURKISH — *sirhirbaz*
YIDDISH — *makhsheyfe*

The Devil carries off a witch   Olaus Magnus (1555)

The Witch and Satan

The thought of a link between witchcraft and Satanism surfaced over six hundred years ago and persists to the present day. In a climate of ignorance and fear promoted by the mass media, the witch comes under attack in a clear case of mistaken identity. The time has come to address a dangerous situation and correct an unfortunate error in judgement.

Followers of witchcraft seldom seek publicity or press for converts. We are content if we can practice our way free of interference. Neither do any of us seek to impose an orthodoxy on others of our persuasion. Within the broad range of this belief system there is room for many paths.

Satanism, however, is essentially alien to our way of thought and over the centuries has caused us considerable harm.

To explain why this is so I must discuss witchcraft in a flat, objective way. This may seem out of place, for to those who can know it at all the craft is revealed in direct mystical experiences. Our own perceptions are the touchstone by which we judge its truths. If what I say about it doesn't jibe with your experience, there is no way I can convince you or prove you wrong.

Nevertheless witchcraft exists in history. It embodies an extremely ancient tradition that was known in one form or another over much of the world. If it represents a survival of Druidism or a cult of the horned god, as some scholars have said, it also was known in the Mysteries of ancient Greece, the following of the Moon goddess, and many other forms.

The arrival of Christianity, often imposed by the sword and the rack, all but extinguished the Old Ways. But they survived in historical accounts that can be interpreted by stripping away the bias, and more importantly they survived through cleverly disguised folklore and secret practice in remote areas where church control was weak. It is this survival that permits us to feel connected with the ancient tradition now that the power of Christianity is fading.

Satanism, on the other hand, springs from Christianity itself and its sources in the Near East. If one reads the Bible as a series of documents produced over time rather than as eternally true revelation, one can see that the nature of Satan underwent an evolution in ancient Palestine just as that of Jahveh (Jehovah) did.

At first Jahveh was one of many gods of different tribes and holy places. He rewarded the worship and sacrifices of the Israelites with prosperity and victory in battle and hence earned their allegiance. He cared little for other peoples. Satan then was another god not much different from Jahveh, perhaps derived from the Baal of other Canaanite tribes. In the book of Job, for instance, Satan appears as an antagonist of Jahveh in a rather friendly contest not unlike a chess match except that it involves a mortal man and his family.

Later, however, the Satan who tempts Jesus in the wilderness is clearly the embodiment of evil. This concept of an evil force opposed to a wholly good God came from the Zoroastrian religion to the East and is plainly expressed in the Essene writings recovered in the so-called Dead Sea scrolls.

As formulated in Manichaeism, this doctrine was denounced as heresy by the fathers of the early Church. They opted instead for the doctrine of an all-powerful God. This choice meant, however, that God must be responsible for evil as well as good. Since then Church leaders have had to explain evil as something necessary for the ultimate working out of God's inscrutable plan for the world, which can be only good. Such a position has not been an easy one to defend through times of war, pestilence and famine, and a strain of Manichaeism has persisted even among the most devout Christians.

Worship of Satan, who, independent of God's will or not, remained in the Scriptures, arose in the Middle Ages as a reaction against Christianity. In its purest form Satanism simply reversed everything Christian. Anything the Church defined as good was evil and vice versa. The ceremonies were a mockery of the Mass and other sacraments. As such Satanism clearly had nothing at all to do with true witchcraft.

The two practices were confused originally not by followers of either one but by the Church, which regarded anything not Christian as devilish. The unspeakable torture of the witch hunts produced confessions that confirmed this view. Sensation-seeking Satanists abetted the confusion when it served to their advantage. Further confusion arose from essentially literary expressions like the Faust story, in which occult powers were conferred in re-

turn for future consignment of the soul to the Christian (but only loosely biblical) hell. The advent of an age that can examine established dogma rationally from without has made it possible to separate strands of un-Christian practice from the anti-Christian.

Satanism, then, can be the worship of an ancient Near Eastern deity; or it can invoke the name of Satan to glorify human primal nature. Or it can be a worship of the evil principle through a conscious inversion of Christian ritual. As such it is not only silly but possibly dangerous.

Why silly? Because evil is not something that can have an authentic and independent existence. Gods are revealed through the experience of a people with their physical and spiritual surroundings. Evil is not a god in this sense. Rather it is an idea — that is, a quality we attribute to things, not something inherent in things.

Evil is not a trait of an object, like a color, that we can perceive through our senses. It is not a disease that

Illustration from Holinshed's *Chronicle* of 1577 (Shakespeare's probable source for the story of Macbeth) portrays the three witches as attractive and noble women unlike the eerie hags of the famous dramatization.

infects us like bacteria, nor is it the gap that appears when a person falls short of meeting some concept of human nature (for who can say what human nature really is?). Nothing is evil in itself; the evil comes from our judging it so.

Of course there can be a general consensus that some action is evil. Most of us would say this of wanton murder, for example. But there can be cases where some of us would say a killing was wanton and others would say it was justified. There can be cases where unlike a few centuries ago, a killing is considered not wanton because the killer was insane and not responsible for the action. In the final analysis, evil is a matter of definition that can change with time, place and people.

The supernatural agencies invoked in true witchcraft are neither good nor evil. They may aid us or harm us or ignore us, but we can call these actions good and evil only in terms of their effects on us. To someone else they may look quite the opposite. The most a witch can honestly say is that he or she believes these agencies are there. "The threefold return for evil done and double that for good deeds, plus one" is an age-old tenet of the craft. Witchcraft really is the quest to discover nature's truths and achieve harmony within it. Nothing can be further from this spirit than Satanism, and it would behoove us to do everything we can to oppose such nonsense.

— CHARLES E. PEPPER

The Old Ways

What is it that calls to us from all ancient things: tangled woods; mossy, lichened stones; secret gardens like Avalon; forgotten paths and long-lost secrets? These things possess a power which flows from their very oldness.

I would say that such experiences are the call of the Old Ways, paths of myth, fable and legend, human dreams, your roots and mine. All ancient things partake of this

mysterious ability to stir one's soul. Jung, the depth psychologist, attributed such feeling to the workings of the unconscious mind; anthropologists refer to them as Numan or Mana; poets call them inspiration. Witches have a better name for what stirs us. We call it magic.

Lay out a deck of Tarot cards and you will feel it breathing out from behind the pale hands and faces of the actors in the Tarot play, once gods and goddesses, now funny little puppets, quaint and hieratic, but still potent. Or open any book of mythology, tales of wonder and lost cults, of Morgana and Arthur, Math and Gwydion, the Tuatha De Danaan, Aradia. Even the contemporary myth — Tolkien's Middle Earth reverberates with the power of the Old Ways, and you will find magic there, for these are the bibles of our hidden gospel.

Yet behind the ceaseless interaction of the elements, rise and fall of stars, birth and death of the year, lie those sources that join our actions to theirs, the great common denominators, the eternal play of birth, love, death, and birth once more, enacted by the unseen Old Ones, lost gods today, but once simply primordial powers. To many of us they are just the Lord and Lady. Whether we care to call them Hu and Cerridwen, Bel and Ioevohe, Pan and Diana, Lucifer and Aradia, Watto and Andred, Cernunnos and Habondia, the archetypes are the same.

Whether our observances are traditional or discovered, handed down within a family or secret group, esoteric book, or even within the fabric of a dream. If they elicit a shiver of wonder and awe — then they are of the Old Ways. Deep will call to deep, power will come down. For at their most fundamental, before they were ever organized into any cult framework, the following could be said of these rites:

The witch and her demon lover

Masked family enroute to the sabbat

Woodcuts from Ulrich Molitor's *De Laniis* (1489), the first printed book about witchcraft

No special class of persons is set apart for their performance. The rites may be performed by anyone, as occasion demands. No special places are set apart for the performance. There are no temples. The rites are magical rather than propitiatory. The desired objects are attained not by propitiating the favor of the divine beings through sacrifice, prayer and praise but by ceremonies which are believed to influence the course of nature directly through a physical resemblance between the rite and the effect.

These are not my words but Sir James Frazer's. His *Golden Bough*, along with Jacob Grimm's *Teutonic Mythology* and *The White Goddess* by Robert Graves are our Testaments.

So if you seek knowledge of the Old Ones, turn to the sun and kiss your hand to the moon; be aware of the sky above your head and the earth beneath your feet, nature's bounty, herbs and all living things. Above all, observe the seasons and the tides. It isn't in human institutions that the true secrets of vision and power are to be looked for, but only in the inwardness of your own being as reflected in nature.

Why go elsewhere when you have what you seek so close at hand?

— PAUL HUSON

The Witch in Early America

From the chapter Salem and Other Witchcraft in *Myths and Legends of Our Own Land*, by Charles M. Skinner, published by J. P. Lippincott in 1896.

The extraordinary persecution recorded at Salem was but a reflection of a kindred insanity in the Old World that was not extirpated until its victims had been counted by thousands.

In 1692 when the madness, which might have been stayed by a seasonable spanking, broke out in Danvers, Massachusetts, the first victim was a wild Irishwoman named Glover. Speedily it involved the neighboring community of Salem.

The mischiefs done by witches included aches and pains, blight of crops, disease of cattle. Children complained of being pricked with thorns and pins (the pins are still preserved in Salem), and if hysterical girls spoke the name of anyone while in flighty talk, the person was virtually sentenced to die. The word of a child of eleven years sufficed to hang, burn, or drown a witch.

Giles Corey, a man of eighty, was condemned to the medieval *peine forte et dure*, his body being crushed beneath a load of rocks and timbers. He refused to plead in court, and when the beams were laid upon him he only cried, "More weight!" The shade of the unhappy victim haunted the scene of his execution for years, and always came to warn people of calamities. Susie Martin of Amesbury, who was hanged, made the rope dance so that it could not be tied until a crow overhead called for a length of vine and the law was executed with that. A child

of five and a dog were also hanged after formal condemnation. Gallows Hill, near Salem, witnessed many sad tragedies, and the old elm tree that stood on Boston Common until 1876 was said to have served as a gallows for witches and Quakers. The accuser of one day was the prisoner of the next, and not even the clergy were safe.

A few escapes were made, like that of a blue-eyed maid of Wenham, whose lover aided her to break out of the wooden jail and carried her safely beyond the Merrimac, finding a home for her among the Quakers; and that of Miss Wheeler, of Salem, who had fallen under suspicion, and whose brothers hurried her into a boat, rowed around Cape Ann, and safely bestowed her in "the witch house" at Pigeon Cove. Many, however, fled to other towns rather than run the risk of accusation, which commonly meant death.

When the wife of Philip English was arrested he, too, asked to share her fate, and both were, through friendly intercession, removed to Boston, where they were allowed to have liberty by day on condition that they would go to jail every night. Just before they were to be taken back to Salem for trial, they went to church and heard the Rev. Joshua Moody preach from the text, "If they persecute you in one city, flee unto another." The good clergyman not only preached goodness, but practiced it, and that night the door of their prison was opened. Furnished with an introduction from Governor Phipps to Governor Fletcher of New York the couple made their way to that settlement and remained there in safe and courteous keeping until the people of Salem had regained their senses. Upon their return to Salem, Mrs. English fell ill and died from the effects of cruelty and anxiety. And although the Rev. Moody was generally commended for his substitution of sense and justice for law, there were many bigots who persecuted him so constantly that he removed to Plymouth.

According to the belief of the time a witch compacted with Satan for the gift of supernatural power, and in return was to give up his soul after his life was over. Satan then gave his ally a familiar in the form of a dog, cat, or other animal, usually small and black. To feed these "familiars" with the blood of the witch was forbidden in English law, which ranked it as a felony; but they were nourished in secret, and by their aid the witch might raise storms, blight crops, abort births, lame cattle, topple over houses, and cause pains, convulsions, and illness. If she desired to hurt a person, a witch made a clay or waxen image in his likeness, and the harms and indignities wreaked on the puppet would be suffered by the one bewitched, a knife or a needle thrust in the waxen body being felt acutely by the living one, no matter how distant he might be. By placing this image in running water, hot sunshine, or near a fire, the living flesh would waste as this melted or dissolved, and the person thus wrought upon would die. This belief is still current among the practitioners of voodoo in the south. The witch, too, had the power of riding the winds, usually with a broomstick for a conveyance, after she had smeared the broom or herself with magic ointment. The flocking of the unhallowed to their sabbats on lonely mountain tops has been minutely described by those who claim to have seen the sight. It was said that only at Christmas a witches' powers failed.

Naturally, the Indians were accused, for they recognized the existence of both good and evil spirits. Their medicine men cured by incantations in the belief that demons were thus driven out of their patients. In the early history of our country the red man was credited by white settlers with powers hardly inferior to those of Oriental and European magicians of the Middle Ages. Cotton Mather detected a relation between Satan and the Indians, and he declared that certain of the Algonquins were trained from boyhood as powahs, powwows, or witches, acquiring powers of second-sight and communion with gods and spirits through abstinence from food and sleep and the observation of certain rites. Their severe discipline made them victims of nervous excitement. The responsibilities of conjuration had on their minds an effect similar to that produced by gases from the rift in Delphi on the Apollonian oracles. The manifestations of insanity or frenzy passed for deific or infernal possession. When John Gibb, a Scot, who had gone mad through religious excitement, was shipped to this country by his tired fellow-countrymen, the Indians hailed him as a more powerful witch than any of their number. Barrow Hill, near Amesbury, was said to be the meeting place for Indian powwows and witches, and at late hours of the night the light of fires gleamed from its top, while shadowy forms glanced athwart it. Old men say that the lights are still there in winter, though modern doubters declare that they are the aurora borealis.

In the Merrimac Valley tales of witchcraft were told: Goody Mose of Rocks Village, who tumbled downstairs

when a big beetle was killed at an evening party some miles away, after it had been bumping into the faces of the company. Goody Sloper, of West Newbury, who went lame directly after a man had struck his axe into the beam of a house that she had bewitched. She recovered her strength and established an improved reputation when, in 1794, she swam out to a capsized boat and rescued two people in peril.

The hill below Easton, Pennsylvania called *Hexenkoph* (witch's head) was described by German settlers as a place of nightly gatherings for the weird ones, who whirled about its top in linked dances and sang in deep tones mingled with laughter. After one of these affairs, in Williams township, a participant was punished for enchanting a twenty-dollar horse. Their sabbats were held more quietly after that. Mom Rinkle, whose rock is pointed out beside the Wissahickon in Philadelphia, "drank dew from acorn cups and had the Evil Eye." Juan Peria of San Mateo, New Mexico, would fly with his fellows to meetings in the mountains in the shape of a fireball. Within the present century an old woman who lived in a hut on the New York Palisades was held to be responsible for local storms and accidents.

Moll Pitcher, a successful sorcerer and fortune teller, figured in obsolete poems, plays, and romances. She was consulted not merely by people of respectability, but by those who had knavish schemes to prosecute and who wanted to learn in advance the outcome of their designs. Many a ship was deserted at the hour of sailing because Moll boded evil of the voyage. She was of average height, big-headed, tangled haired, long-nosed, and had searching green eyes. The sticks she carried were cut from a hazel bush that hung athwart a brook.

As a citizen of New Haven was riding home — this was at the time of the goings on at Salem — he saw shapes of women near his horse's head, whispering earnestly

together and keeping time with the trot of his animal without effort of their own. "In the name of God, tell me who you are," cried the traveler, and at the name of God they vanished. Next day the man's orchard was shaken by viewless hands and the fruit thrown down.

In the early days of this century, a skinny old woman known as Aunt Woodward lived by herself in a log cabin at Minot Corner, Maine, enjoying the awe of all the people in that isolated burg. On her account people moved around little at night and one poor girl was in mortal fear lest by mysterious arts she should be changed into a white horse. One citizen kept Aunt Woodward away from his house by nailing a horseshoe to his door, while another took the force out of her spells by keeping a branch of "round wood" at his threshold. At night, it was believed, Auntie enjoyed haunting a big square house in town where the ghost of a murdered infant was often heard crying. By day she laid charms on her neighbor's provisions and utensils, and turned their cream to buttermilk. In spite of all her mischief, the witch died in bed.

Witchcraft in America Today

America was settled during the seventeenth century as a witch persecution swept over Europe and the British Isles. It is not surprising that many arrivals to these shores brought with them certain secret traditions and memories belonging to some ancient source now dimmed by distance and the mists of time.

Solitaries

All across America, in tiny hamlets and in large cities, scores of solitary witches quietly practice their craft. Contrary to a prevalent notion, these individuals do not consider witchcraft a religion. Such a concept — the acknowledgment and worship of deities in concert with others — has no relation to the art or work which these witches perform. And while they view the emergence of neo-covens with more than passing interest, few are moved to join the groups. Perhaps the idea of rules and dogma, initiation rites and paraphernalia is not appealing to them.

Words are but symbols of thought and define in a limited way the nature and variety of solitary witchcraft practitioners. For reasons too complicated to sort out, a deep attraction for the unknown, the mysterious, the occult has always been part of their nature. Few witches can recall the precise moment when a kind of clarity lighted their minds and a spontaneous awareness took place. Something moved them to develop certain powers, as yet unidentified by science, often regarded as illusory, but undeniably present to varying degrees in all human beings. Mastering the art of harnessing nature's gifts is an exciting and rewarding activity. Success often depends more on instinct and feelings rather than strict discipline and adherence to precepts. Some novices are fortunate enough to have a family member to guide their quest. Others find their way alone.

Solitary witches are far and away the largest body of occultists working in America today. They belong to no particular background, race, color, tradition, social class or age group. These witches may use their powers for good and for evil, too, because they are human with both positive and negative motivations. However, the good usually outweighs the ill, for wisdom often accompanies the development of mystical power. The effort involved is too great to be wasted upon an unworthy cause. And while some solitaries will acknowledge that they practice witchcraft, others merely allow that they have an interest in metaphysical matters. So independent is the nature of the solitary witch that any attempt to categorize one is doomed to fail. Let's just say they were, are, and will be fulfilling a natural inclination by responding to life in this particular fashion.

Traditional Covens

During the early years of the twentieth century, groups of occultists worked together in America. Many were witches. Their activity was cloaked in secrecy, but usually involved the raising of psychic power for spiritualistic or healing purposes. It is true that those blessed with spiritual gifts can often perform extraordinary feats in concert with their peers. Due to low profiles, it is now impossible to document whether or not they celebrated religious rites. A Scottish coven in western Kentucky observed the four traditional holidays and met under the full moon, but a description of the proceedings more resembles that of a Victorian seance than a religious festivity. Similarly, a Spanish Basque coven in Rhode Island practiced techniques of mental magic together while calling on the power of the elements rather than paying homage to a divinity. But these are only two examples of traditional covens in which religion played a minor role. Covens met in Massachusetts, Virginia, Maryland, Florida — some dating back to colonial times. There the story may have been quite different. Witches seek no converts and cherish privacy. We can say little about them beyond acknowledging the fact that they did and do exist. Within recent years, evidence concerning traditional covens from a variety of sources has surfaced in nearly every state in the union. Whether they meet to raise power or honor the Old Gods is not known. They keep their secrets.

Neo-Covens

Dr. Margaret Murray's book, *The Witch Cult in Western Europe*, published in 1921, was a primary inspiration for the revival of coven structure in contemporary witchcraft. The controversial work, an anathema to academicians, theorized that the witch cult brought to light during the era of persecution was the survival of a pre-Christian religious expression. In 1954, occultist Gerald Gardner wrote *Witchcraft Today*, a book in which he detailed the activity of a coven to which he belonged that traced its origins back to the Dionysian Mysteries of ancient Greece. Drawing on many sources, Gardner evolved a system of worship known as Wicca. Most adherents would agree that Gardnerian Wicca has much in common with Dr. Murray's Dianic cult of pagan days: worship of the universal creative forces as symbolized by the Horned God and Moon Goddess. In America today, especially in large cities and their suburbs, there are many Gardnerian covens but more often than not they favor variations on his theme. Few retain the practice of nude rites, or as Gardner termed it "sky-clad." Americans seem to prefer wearing robes when they worship.

The Alexandrian branch of Wicca has not had the acceptance here that the group enjoys in England. Founded by Alex Sanders in the 1950's, its adherents celebrate fertility rites similar to the Gardnerian and worship the same deities. But Alexandrians are more inclined to pursue aspects of ceremonial magic—or what may be termed the "science of witchcraft" so appealing to the Victorian mind.

Most neo-covens have no links with modern British witchcraft. Some have evolved naturally from a nucleus of occult devotees. Others are offshoots of traditional covens led by an adept versed in the Old Ways. Hungarian, Italian, French, Welsh, and Finnish groups are among those represented. Another branch of group-affiliated "witches" draw inspiration from journalistic sources and often display a high degree of internal strife. Perhaps this is part of all beginnings.

Over our years of publication, we have come to know witches of every persuasion. They have found kinship in the Almanac and have been moved to write and tell us so. From their letters, a composite picture emerges of a warm, light-hearted spirit, dignified and courageous. Our correspondents are fair-minded and more often than not share a deep devotion to wild nature and our animal kin. Our adepts cherish privacy and count the individual as infinitely more important than society as a whole. All facets of the occult world fascinate them and whether they regard witchcraft as an art, a science, a religion, or simply a way of life — they are a constant source of joy to us.

The Planetary Hours   Augsburg (1490)

No one knows why the planetary hours do not proceed in the same order as the days of the week. Study this old German woodcut and you'll be able to remember the proper sequence. There's Mars in full armor at twelve o'clock high and following him, the majestic Sun; next comes Venus holding her arrow of desire and after her, Mercury with his staff and serpent. The wistful Moon, old Saturn with his scythe, and vital Jupiter bearing a flowering bough complete the circle.

Albertus Magnus, the thirteenth-century Bavarian philosopher, first established the type of magical work governed by each heavenly body.

MARS: Growth, strength, health, defense, sex life, matrimony, hostility
SUN: Illumination, energy, action, hope, self-expression, motivation
VENUS: Love, desire, harmony, constancy, friendship, unity, beauty
MERCURY: Wisdom, intelligence, opinion, fear, debt, nervous tension
MOON: Enchantment, dreams, wishes, moods, plans, habits, ways
SATURN: Peace, divination, change, ambition, progress, patience, loss
JUPITER: Law, honor, expansion, humor, wealth, adventure, bold quests

20

2 OF TIME AND CHANGE

Time was invented by man, not by nature, and long before clocks existed man measured his days by the sun and the moon; his seasons by the softness of the land, the constellations of the sky.

Time was invented by man to chart nature's natural rhythm but if all the clocks were to stop the rhythm would continue unchanged.

The Planetary Hours

Telling time is an arbitrary measure. Even today, despite our strict adherence to an hour's passage, the real timekeeper is still the stars above as defined and regulated by a series of observatories all over the world.

During the Renaissance, when clocks replaced sundials and hourglasses, sixty-minute intervals became significant in ritual magic. Each hour was assigned to a planet's rule and ceremonies were performed accordingly.

The distinguished occultist Arthur Edward Waite dismissed as absurd the system of planetary hours presented in the famed *Key of Solomon* because it was based on sunrise and sunset. Waite preferred the more precise table attributed to Peter of Abano in the grimoire *Heptameron*, or *Magical Elements*. Most ceremonial magicians agree, for this chart applies to the individual life experience clocked from midnight to midnight and is not subject to change by zone shifts or daylight saving schemes.

HOURS OF THE NIGHT
from midnight to noon

	Sunday	Monday	Tuesday	Wednesday	Thursday	Friday	Saturday
1st	Sun	Moon	Mars	Mercury	Jupiter	Venus	Saturn
2nd	Venus	Saturn	Sun	Moon	Mars	Mercury	Jupiter
3rd	Mercury	Jupiter	Venus	Saturn	Sun	Moon	Mars
4th	Moon	Mars	Mercury	Jupiter	Venus	Saturn	Sun
5th	Saturn	Sun	Moon	Mars	Mercury	Jupiter	Venus
6th	Jupiter	Venus	Saturn	Sun	Moon	Mars	Mercury
7th	Mars	Mercury	Jupiter	Venus	Saturn	Sun	Moon
8th	Sun	Moon	Mars	Mercury	Jupiter	Venus	Saturn
9th	Venus	Saturn	Sun	Moon	Mars	Mercury	Jupiter
10th	Mercury	Jupiter	Venus	Saturn	Sun	Moon	Mars
11th	Moon	Mars	Mercury	Jupiter	Venus	Saturn	Sun
12th	Saturn	Sun	Moon	Mars	Mercury	Jupiter	Venus

HOURS OF THE DAY
from noon to midnight

	Sunday	Monday	Tuesday	Wednesday	Thursday	Friday	Saturday
1st	Jupiter	Venus	Saturn	Sun	Moon	Mars	Mercury
2nd	Mars	Mercury	Jupiter	Venus	Saturn	Sun	Moon
3rd	Sun	Moon	Mars	Mercury	Jupiter	Venus	Saturn
4th	Venus	Saturn	Sun	Moon	Mars	Mercury	Jupiter
5th	Mercury	Jupiter	Venus	Saturn	Sun	Moon	Mars
6th	Moon	Mars	Mercury	Jupiter	Venus	Saturn	Sun
7th	Saturn	Sun	Moon	Mars	Mercury	Jupiter	Venus
8th	Jupiter	Venus	Saturn	Sun	Moon	Mars	Mercury
9th	Mars	Mercury	Jupiter	Venus	Saturn	Sun	Moon
10th	Sun	Moon	Mars	Mercury	Jupiter	Venus	Saturn
11th	Venus	Saturn	Sun	Moon	Mars	Mercury	Jupiter
12th	Mercury	Jupiter	Venus	Saturn	Sun	Moon	Mars

A Week of Days

A week of days is a very old way to reckon the passage of time. Some say the interval is based on the phases of the moon, which occur about seven days apart. Another theory holds that the days were named for the heavenly bodies observed by the ancients to move across the sky: the sun, the moon, and the five planets which could be seen with the naked eye.

The rising and setting of the sun and the moon, our primary luminaries, had been regarded with awe from the beginning. Traditionally they have come to represent the first and second day of the week cycle, or Sunday and Monday. The planets (the word is derived from the Greek meaning "wandering") were first recognized by the Chaldeans, the knowledge spreading to Greece and Rome during the centuries preceding the Christian era. The "wanderers" came to be identified with Roman deities possessing similar characteristics. The red color of Mars (Tuesday) was likened to the god of war. The messenger Mercury (Wednesday) moved swiftest. Jupiter's size matched the most powerful of gods, while the beauty of the planet Venus was in keeping with that of the goddess of love. The faintly discernible rings around Saturn (Saturday) linked the planet with that god's symbol, the wheel. For over four hundred years, Roman customs influenced all peoples who came under the sway of the Empire. But in the homely matter of naming days, our English language shows that the conquered tribes used the names of Norse rather than Roman deities. The exception is Saturday; Teutonic folk had no equivalent for Saturn, Roman god of seed sowing.

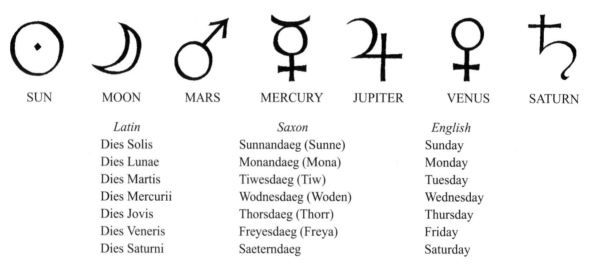

| | SUN | MOON | MARS | MERCURY | JUPITER | VENUS | SATURN |

Latin	*Saxon*	*English*
Dies Solis	Sunnandaeg (Sunne)	Sunday
Dies Lunae	Monandaeg (Mona)	Monday
Dies Martis	Tiwesdaeg (Tiw)	Tuesday
Dies Mercurii	Wodnesdaeg (Woden)	Wednesday
Dies Jovis	Thorsdaeg (Thorr)	Thursday
Dies Veneris	Freyesdaeg (Freya)	Friday
Dies Saturni	Saeterndaeg	Saturday

Years of Witchcraft

During the Middle Ages when literacy began to reach all levels of society, a method of assigning a classification to each year was recorded. Its origin may have been Old Irish, although no one knows for sure. Beginning with the sign of Aries, the time of rebirth in our hemisphere, the years run in cycles of nine. Their sequence is as follows:

2003 — SUN	2006 — FIRE	2009 — PLANT
2004 — MOON	2007 — AIR	2010 — ANIMAL
2005 — EARTH	2008 — WATER	2011 — STONE

Soothsayers have used the sequence as an aid in foretelling events. Dream Books, so popular in the 1930's, called it a tradition of witchcraft. Perhaps its most important function is to keep us aware of change. No year is ever quite like any other. Each brings its gifts and claims its tolls.

By working backwards you can find your own birth year's designation. It is said that if your zodiac sign's element is the same as that of your birth year, your passage through life will be marked by good fortune. Should they conflict, you must expect disharmony and be prepared to counteract it. This is usually accomplished by the use of charms, spells and talismans.

Those born in the years of the basic kingdoms will possess special powers: STONE — sound logic and wise judgement; PLANT — the gift of intuitive reasoning; and ANIMAL — the capacity for abstract thought. People born in these years will pay a high price for their abilities. Although often successful by worldly standards, they may be denied personal happiness and contentment.

A man born in a year of the Sun will be strongly masculine. A woman of the Moon is gentle, subtle and mysterious. Together they form a perfect union; other marriages pale by comparison. This is part of a very old wisdom.

Beginnings

Have you ever wondered why January 1 is celebrated as the beginning of a new year? Actually our current New Year's Day is of relatively recent origin. Britain and her colonies heralded the new year on March 21 until the year 1752.

It was traditional in Western Europe for many years to mark the beginning of a new year with the spring — the time when day and night are of equal duration at the vernal or spring equinox. Earlier rural societies had reckoned time by the seasons, months by the moon phases and days by the setting of the sun. The ancients considered the interval of darkness from sunset to dawn as the start of the day. And just as the nighttime of the womb preceded birth, so the sun's retreat and dark winter was the prelude to spring. The Celtic tribes marked November Eve as the starting point of the year. But Western traditions spring from a very confusing variety of forces and influences.

The ancient Egyptians observed that the brilliant star Sirius (Sothis) appeared once a year just before dawn on the eastern horizon. This auspicious event coincided with the annual rise of the Nile, signifying the start of agricultural activity and a natural beginning of a new year. Neither the appearance of Sirius nor the time of flooding were dependable points of reference, so an Egyptian New Year's Day could occur in early June or much later. Despite the lack of precision, the Egyptians did devise a solar calendar of twelve months while the rest of their neighbors in the Near East depended on the more primitive lunar calendar.

The spring or autumnal equinoxes served most of the ancient civilizations as the starting point of a new year. The Hebrews, according to the Talmud, ushered in a new year at springtime in Palestine, but in Babylonia the holiday came to be celebrated in early autumn, a custom retained by Jews to the present day.

The Greeks combined solar and lunar time. A new year began on the first sight of the new moon after summer solstice (June 21). The following months, or moons, were named after gods or the seasonal festivals held to honor them.

The Romans reckoned time in similar fashion to the Greeks but their new year began at the appearance of the new moon closest to the spring equinox. They named their months: *Martius, Aprilis, Maius, Junius, Quintilis, Sexitis, September, October, November, December, Januarius, Februarius.* In forthright Roman style, half the months were numbered — *Quintilis*, the fifth month, to *December*, the tenth month. Others reflected seasonal activities and festivals. Mars was honored in *Martius*, Juno in *Junius* and Janus in *Januarius*.

The two-faced Janus was strictly a Roman god and the origins of his worship predate Etruscan times. His temple was a gate or doorway symbolizing "good beginnings." Representations of Janus show one face looking to the past and the other to the future. The influence of Janus eventually led the Romans to celebrate the turn of the year during the time of his festival in *Januarius* or January. Ancient records show that in 153 B. C., January 9 was designated as New Year's Day in Rome. But Julius Caesar changed that.

Caesar, with the aid of the Alexandrian astronomer Sosigenes, reformed the calendar system. As a result of Caesar's decree that the calendar year should agree with the solar year, the system of leap years was instituted: that is, one day was added to every fourth year. Caesar gave the fifth month his own name (July) and Sexitis, the sixth, became August for the Emperor Augustus. The first year under the Julian calendar was 46 B.C. and officially began on March 21.

Improvement though it was, the Julian calendar didn't entirely rectify an eleven minute disparity between official and natural calendars, which by the year 1582 amounted to about ten days. In that year Pope Gregory XIII ordained that the ten extra days be dropped from the calendar, and to ensure that the discrepancy was not repeated modified the Julian calendar to eliminate leap years falling on centennial years unless they were divisible by four hundred. Thus 1600 and 2000 are leap years but 1700, 1800 and 1900 were not. Pope Gregory determined that the year should begin on January 1.

The Gregorian calendar was immediately adopted by Spain, Portugal and the Catholic states of Germany and France (which up to that time had celebrated New Year's on April 1), with Protestant Germany following suit about a century later. Britain and its colonies, resisting any and all Roman Catholic influences, continued using the old calendar until 1752, when by Act of Parliament it switched to the Gregorian system and January 1 marked the beginning of a new year.

A Change in the Weather

Witches, long recognized as having sympathetic knowledge and understanding of the forces of nature, have their own natural prognosticators in order to foretell a change in the weather.

FAIR

Red sky at evening
Crescent moon with horns up
Owl hooting after midnight
Mist in the valley
Red lightning
Gnats sporting
Clouds like wool
Evening rainbow

RAIN

Yellow streaks in sunset sky
Frogs croaking
Dark mist over the moon
Twinkling stars
Red sky at morning
Leaves showing their backs
Crows agitating their wings
Cows reclining
Sheep frisking wantonly

WIND

Fiery sun at setting
Sharp horns on a sickle moon
Sea surging
Thunder in the morning
Leaves rustling in the forest
Spider webs in the air
Thistledown floating on water
Herons flying above the clouds
Ducks flapping their wings

STORM

Shooting stars
Wolf howling
Pale sun at rising
Finches and sparrows chirping at dawn
Birds fleeing from the sea
Bees not venturing from the hive
Mice skipping around
Dogs rolling on the ground

HARD WINTER

Trees holding their leaves
Tough apple skin
Narrow band on woolly bear caterpillar
Early departure of birds to the south
Wild geese flying low
Long shaggy hair on horses and cattle
Weeds growing high
Bountiful crop of acorns
Large store of honey

A sorcerer offers winds for sale   Olaus Magnus (1555)

The Winds of Change

Egyptians deified the wind and called him Shu. The Greeks, seafarers much concerned with winds, named a god for each of the compass points and appointed as regent a god called Aeolus.

North	Boreas
Northeast	Kaikias
East	Apeliotes
Southeast	Euros
South	Notos
Southwest	Liponotos
West	Zephyros
Northwest	Skiron

Through the history of witchcraft we find many references to the winds. The illustration above depicts a Finnish witch offering to sell to becalmed sailors winds bound up in a rope with three knots. The legend tells us that when the first knot was unloosed a light breeze sprang up; a second undone brought a gale; the third, a tempest. Estonian witches, with proper ceremony, would thrust a knife into a block of wood from the direction they wished the wind to blow. In Scotland a witch raised the wind by dipping a rag in a fast-running brook and beating it three times on a square stone while chanting:

> *Upon this stone I knock a rag*
> *To raise the wind in the lady's name,*
> *It shall not lie or cease and die*
> *Until I please again.*

English witches could whistle up the wind. In the first light of dawn, facing the direction from which they wished the wind to come, they would summon it with three long, clear whistles blown between the first and fourth fingers of the right hand.

Among Aradia's gifts of power to the witch, as recounted in Leland's translation of the *Vangelo*, or the Gospel of the Witches, we find the ability to understand the voice of the wind. The symbolic meaning is clear. The motion of human thought, opinions and values are like the winds: they rise, shift, back and veer; they prevail, they freshen into gales only to die again. Change alone endures.

A Second Wind

When courage fails and all seems lost, a witch ritually summons a second wind, the reserve force that renews hope. The simple act of lighting a candle can be raised to the level of a sacred rite when performed at the right time and in an appropriate atmosphere. Optimism belongs to the mind's domain, the mysterious realm where a change of attitude makes the difference between success and failure, happiness and misery. To lift the spirit is the way to recover normal power and balance.

The first step is the decision to take action. Plan the ceremony and allow yourself enough time to enjoy anticipation. Anticipation is an important factor in all endeavors. Challenge your mind with the necessity of

choices — where, when, and in what manner — to increase its liveliness. Anxiety and despair deaden human facilities. The mind can become lost in a downward spiral of repetitive thoughts. Determine to banish negativity for one hour.

Choose a quiet, comfortable place where privacy is assured. Within the time of a waxing moon, from dark to full, sit before a lighted candle with a flame at eye level. Breathe gently as you fix your gaze on the brightest part of the flame. Return to childhood and remember what it was like to play the game of pretend. Make believe the candle flame is something that shines deep within you — call it heart or soul or spirit — a thing unseen yet comprehensible, intangible yet knowable. It is there and it is yours just waiting to be acknowledged and reclaimed. With its image clear in your mind's eye, cup your hand around the flame and softly blow it out.

Hold the memory of its glow as a source of courage whenever you need a refreshing second wind.

Seasons of Being

Autumn is familiarly the season of color, winter is the season of form, spring the season of texture, and summer the season of motion.

— HENRY BESTON

The four natural divisions of the year have always been a source of inspiration. Ancient myths portray the winter as a blue-faced hag venting her rage on the earth. Spring is a beautiful maiden released from imprisonment. Summer's fruitfulness is celebrated with joyful feasts, and autumn's melancholy is relieved by the glory of harvest.

Our forebears found a wonderful harmony in the color, form, texture, and motion of the changing seasons. Is it by living close to the soil and performing the duties required by it that we gain not only sustenance but peace of mind and heart?

Perceiving the beauty of certainty and change, medieval art and literature charted the pace of the seasons. All of Europe and the British Isles shared the rhythm of the year.

March	*Here I set my things to spring,*
April	*And here I hear the birds sing.*
May	*I am light as bird on bough,*
June	*And I weed my corn well enow.*
July	*With my scythe my mead I mow,*
August	*And here I shear my corn full low.*
September	*With my flail I earn my bread,*
October	*And here I sow my wheat so red.*
November	*Now is the time I kill my swine,*
December	*And at Yule I drink red wine.*
January	*By this fire I warm my hands,*
February	*And with my spade I delve my lands.*

English manuscript, 1475

March	Turning soil in manorial garden
April	Peasants milking cows and tending sheep
May	Youths and maidens drift in pleasure skiff
June	Shearing sheep
July	Making hay
August	Mowing and sheaving grain
September	Ploughing and seeding a field
October	A bull is sold in the village
November	Flax is scutched and hackled
December	A pig is jugulated outside an inn
January	Men sup and warm themselves before a fire
February	Peasants prune vines and break ground

The Da Costa Hours, Flemish, 1520

March	Ploughing
April	Nobles meeting on the lawn
May	Nobles in May Procession
June	Peasants making hay
July	Peasants shearing sheep
August	Nobles hunting
September	Harvesting grapes
October	Ploughing and sowing grain
November	Shaking down nuts to feed pigs
December	Hunters with dogs seek boar
January	Nobles feasting and jousting

Les Tres Riches Heures du Duc de Berry, French, 1416

Almanacs

An almanac is a guide to the changing seasons, a means designed long ago to quicken awareness of the natural world and, in our case, the unseen world beyond normal sensory limits.

The word "almanac" may derive from the Arabic, meaning "to reckon," or from the Saxon *al-mon-aght*, a name given to Norse runic clogs (carved sticks of wood) detailing a year's progression. It is not until the end of the thirteenth century that the Latin form *almanach* appears. But making a record of prognostications for a coming year has been a human activity since earliest time. Among Egyptian scrolls in the British Museum is a fragment of an almanac indicating specific dates for religious festivals as well as lucky and unlucky days. The parchment *fasti* of the Romans, dating from the reign of Augustus, are remarkably similar in form to modern almanacs.

During the Middle Ages in Europe, artists were receiving royal commissions to embellish manuscript calendars known as Books of Days. The artistic triumphs on vellum set the style for a more humble version on paper — the common almanac form. The invention of printing in the fifteenth century heralded a steady advance in literacy. Almanacs, cheap to produce, soon achieved wide circulation and gained increasing influence. To the farmer, the slender volumes became a source for discovering favorable agricultural days. To the rest of the population, the little books provided a guide to daily action, for the form had expanded to include astrological predictions.

In no country was the almanac more successful and varied than in France. Writers, poets, sculptors, dancers, merchants and soldiers all had issues devoted to their interests. The famed Almanach de Gotha, published in Germany since 1793, features genealogical information regarding the royal families of Europe.

Perhaps the earliest almanac in the English language is an illuminated manuscript of 1386, but the oldest printed specimen is Richard Pynson's *Shepheards' Kalendar*, dated 1497. By 1600 there had been well over 600 different almanacs printed in England. A figure of at least six million has been estimated as the total production of almanacs in the seventeenth century. Francis Moore is the most famous of English almanac-makers; his first number appeared in 1700. Under the title of *Old Moore's Almanac*, publication continues to the present day.

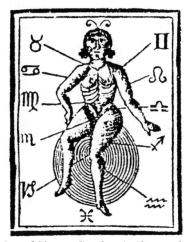

The Man of Signs, *Goodwin's Almanack*, 1821

With the Age of Reason came a spate of mock almanacs. The first American effort in this satirical vein was *Poor Robin*, named after its English predecessor and compiled by Benjamin Franklin's brother in Newport, Rhode Island in 1728. Under the pseudonym Richard Saunders, the statesman himself wrote and published his own review, *Poor Richard's Almanack*, from 1732 to 1758. Franklin's wit and sagacity made it the first publication to achieve success on both sides of the Atlantic. The number of different almanacs published at various times in America is astonishing, with over 14,000 titles cited in the Library of Congress. America's oldest existing periodical is *The Old Farmer's Almanac*, established in 1792 by Robert E. Thomas.

Moses Coit Tyler in his *History of American Literature* is derisive of those who "turn away in lofty scorn from the almanac. That most despised, most prolific, most indispensable of books served our ancestors not only as a calendar, but as a compendium of science, biography, history, wit, and useful daily information. No book has been more universally read, or more highly valued, or more serviceable to its day and generation."

27

Wild Kingdom   Tobias Stimmer (1576)

3   ABOUT ANIMALS

The Kingdom of Nature is threefold: animal, vegetable, and mineral.

Ancient Egyptian civilization, unique in world history, acknowledged kinship with all living creatures. Even more significantly, the society assigned spiritual significance to many members of the animal kingdom. Combining qualities of human and hawk to symbolically represent the ruler of earth and sky, the Egyptians worshiped the great sun god Ra. If no other evidence existed, the art produced over a three thousand year span confirms the honor bestowed on all forms of life. With skillful sensitivity, artists captured the character of each species: a superb brush drawing of a heron on a tomb wall, the majestic avenue of rams at Karnak, the eternal beauty of Queen Nefertiti's face, or the quiet serenity of a sculptured cat. Egyptians made no distinction between humans and other animals, believing that all creatures on earth belonged to one family. "The Hebrews, Greeks, and Romans never understood the logical conception which underlay the reverence with which the Egyptians regarded animals, and as a result they grossly misrepresented their religion," stated E. A. Wallis Budge, of the British Museum.

Cats and dogs were household companions of the ancient Egyptians, beloved, pampered, and honored at their death. "A cat's natural demise required the family to shave their eyebrows," according to Herodotus, "but if a dog die, they shave the whole body and head." The animals were embalmed and buried "amid the greatest manifestations of grief by those to whom they belonged."

Night of the Jackal

Winter, the night of the year, belonged to the Egyptian god Anubis. Symbolized as a jackal — a nocturnal animal and wild member of the dog family — his primary function in Egyptian myths was as a protector and faithful guardian.

One of the oldest gods, Anubis played many roles. He was Lord of the Nether World, god of embalming, and judge of the dead, for it was Anubis who held the scales of truth to determine the virtue of the deceased. By the time the Osirian mortuary ritual was established, Anubis was portrayed with a human body. Only his jackal-

28

head identified his character.

Among the treasures from Tutankhamen's tomb is a life-sized statue of a jackal. There he is, black and lean, recumbent yet alert; an ideal representation of a guardian being. Few captured the quality of animals with such fidelity as did the ancient Egyptians.

The Egyptians identified Anubis with the constellation we know as the Little Dipper. The Romans called it Ursa Minor, the Little Bear, but also named it Cynosura, the dog's tail. This pattern of stars contains the single most important celestial body in the night sky — the North or Pole Star. As a constant guide to due north, it served humans well. So in the form of a constellation (possibly the original concept), Anubis is steadfast and dependable.

Many of us across America share our home with a fine black dog. Many more successfully use the image of Anubis as a visualization focus when casting spells of protection. And when the winter seems especially long and your peace of mind feels threatened, take time to walk out on a clear moonless night. Look to the north and count out the seven stars of his constellation while you say: *Anubis, the good oxherd, bring in the light to me, for thou shalt give protection to me here tonight!*

This prayer comes from the Leyden Papyrus, an Egyptian document of practical magic dating from the third century of the common era.

The Black Dog

British folklore is rich with tales of a ghostly black dog that appears out of nowhere to guide and protect a traveler passing through a dark wood or other dangerous terrain. When the journey ends and safety is assured, the guardian dog vanishes into thin air. One such tale appeared in *Memorial of a Quiet Life* by Augustus Hare, nineteenth-century English travel writer. A young man named Johnnie Greenwood, responding to an emergency, was required to cross a mile of dense forest to reach his destination.

"At the entrance of the wood a large black dog joined him, and pattered along by his side. He could not make out where it came from, but it never left him, and when the wood grew so dark that he could not see it, he still heard it pattering beside him. When he emerged from the wood, the dog disappeared, and he could not tell where it had gone to. Well, Johnnie fulfilled his obligation, and set out to return the same way. At the entrance of the wood, the dog joined him, and pattered along beside him as before; but it never touched him, and he never spoke to it, and again, as he emerged from the wood, it ceased to be there.

"Years after, two condemned prisoners in York Jail told the chaplain that they had intended to rob and murder Johnnie that night in the wood, but that he had a large dog with him, and when they saw that, they felt that Johnnie and the dog together would be too much for them."

The Wonder of Cats

Egyptians chose the domestic cat to symbolize Bast, goddess of beauty, pleasure, music, and magic. She had attributes of both sun and moon, but essentially Bast was regarded as nocturnal, a goddess of mystery and keeper of lunar secrets.

While the link between the cat and the occult is often credited solely to its deification by the Egyptians, it is interesting to note that the chariot of Freya, Norse goddess of love and beauty, was traditonally drawn by two gray cats. Another reason may be the ancient Celtic belief that

a cat's eyes are the windows through which human beings may explore an inner world.

Whatever the origin of the connection between the feline nature and magic, cats and witches have enjoyed a long association. Nocturnal creatures of evil repute, both suffer the consequences of falsely inspired fear along with being called "she" regardless of gender. Both provoke unreasonable hostility merely by being true to their own nature. But misfortune alone does not hold them together. An archetypal kinship and a deep, genuine affection are evident in most cat-witch relationships. Many people who assume that the cat is remote and aloof are surprised to see it behave like a friendly puppy in the company of a witch.

Not every witch is a cat lover, nor is every cat qualified to be a psychic aide. But should cats hold for you a special fascination, you would do well to engage one as a familiar spirit. Let instinct alone guide your choice. Breed, color or sex are not determining factors. The potential familiar will possess a mystic quality to be inwardly sensed rather than outwardly seen.

For establishing strong personal ties, it is not sufficient to merely observe the ancient ceremony of mixing a drop of your own blood in its first saucer of milk or of eating together from the same plate. These acts are said to "strengthen the psychic bond between ye." Such rituals cannot replace time, patience and acts of kindness, which lead to mutual love and respect.

Here, from an eighteenth-century book of shadows, are instructions for the training of the cat to occult use:

To be performed every evening, at the same time, in the same place. Adapt the cat to sit close by you, facing the east. Stroke gently but firmly with love in your hands until its purrs and your breathing are heard as one sound. Now you and your cat possess the same will, your eyes will see alike, your thoughts will travel together. The time has come to work spells and cast enchantments for power is doubled through the agency of your familiar.

Keeping a Cat

A witch talks to animals, especially to cats. The sound of the human voice has the power to comfort in crisis, cheer the lonely and evoke a marvelous response of affection and understanding in the feline. The effort is worthwhile, for cats are loyal friends and delightful companions.

People who are not familiar with cats but would like to be should know that soft-toned, soothing, matter-of-fact conversation is what a cat likes best. And above all, use their names.

T. S. Eliot, in his superb collection of poems about cats, *Old Possum's Book of Practical Cats*, tells us that a cat has three different names. One is sensible, another peculiar, and the third is the one only the cat knows, his "deep and inscrutable singular Name." Although Eliot concludes "no human research can discover" that secret name, no harm comes from trying. Watch your cat's reaction to a variety of sounds. Some say they respond to sibilants in English: s, z, ch, sh, zh or j. Yet cats are so individual no firm rules ever apply, only guidelines. Should the name you choose please the cat, you'll find that within a matter of days he or she will come immediately when called. Cats learn quickly if they so choose.

Cats are creatures of habit. Despite reports to the contrary, they do have a keen sense of the passage of time, and they like to eat, sleep, romp, or sit in your lap at regular intervals. Any break in an established routine distresses them. Most felines prefer not to travel. Upon arrival in new quarters, always allow a cat to explore the strange territory without interruption. Nothing annoys a cat more than being followed. If for safety's sake you must capture one, the best policy is to pretend you just happen to be going in the same direction and focus your attention away from it. Like as not it will come over to see what you are doing. You can count on a cat's curiosity.

Once you've tamed a cat you must take responsibility for its well being. Provide an environment to suit its needs: a high perch for a safe retreat, a strong scratching-post, warm nests for naps and toys for amusement. These, along with fresh water, good food, proper litter pan, lots of love and conversation should satisfy the most particular feline. And don't forget an occasional catnip treat.

Catnip you grow yourself is vastly superior to the commercial product. It is a hardy plant, easily grown from seed, and quite as happy in a pot on a fire escape in Manhattan as in an herb garden in Kansas. Most cats enjoy both fresh and dried flowering heads and leaves. There are always exceptions. Kittens are apt to be repelled by the strong mint odor. But in general a whiff of catnip is enough to delight a cat. Some chew, others just sniff, and if you have more than one cat, mock battles will ensue with lots of good-natured cuffing and rolling. All in all, catnip excites action and is a cheerful tonic to the spirit.

In Praise of Cats

The French have probably said more memorable things about cats than any other race. Some Gallic observations:

When I play with my cat, who knows but that she regards me more as a plaything than I do her?
— MONTAIGNE

Cats know not how to pardon.
— JEAN DE LA FONTAINE

The cat is the only animal which accepts the comforts but rejects the bondage of domesticity.
— COMTE DE BUFFON

Watch a cat when it enters a room for the first time. It is not quiet for a moment, it trusts nothing until it has examined and made acquaintance with everything.
— JEAN JACQUES ROUSSEAU

Illustrations by Elizabeth Pepper

Cats always know whether people like or dislike them. They do not always care enough to do anything about it.

— WINIFRED CARRIERE

I love my cats because I love my home, and little by little they become its visible soul.

— JEAN COCTEAU

I love in the cat that independent and most ungrateful temper which prevents it from attaching itself to anyone; the indifference with which it passes from the salon to the housetop.

— CHATEAUBRIAND

It is a difficult matter to gain the affection of a cat. He is a philosophical, methodical animal, tenacious of his own habits, fond of order and neatness, and disinclined to extravagant sentiment. He will be your friend, if he finds you worthy of friendship, but not your slave.

— THEOPHILE GAUTIER

By associating with the cat, one only risks becoming richer.

— COLETTE

The cat is utterly sincere.

— FERNAND MERY

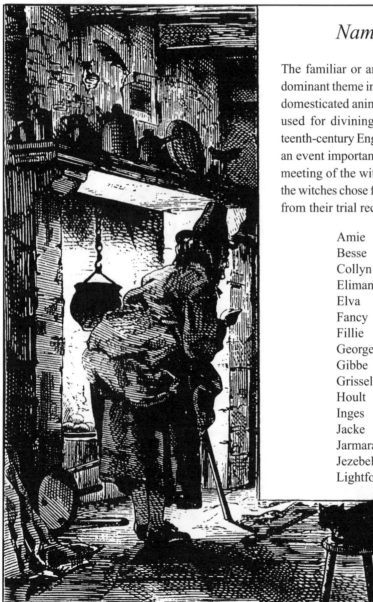

Naming Familiars

The familiar or animal companion to a witch is a dominant theme in the history of witchcraft. A small domesticated animal, most often a dog or a cat, was used for divining and working magic. In seventeenth-century England the naming of a familiar was an event important enough to call for an esbat — a meeting of the witches' coven. Some of the names the witches chose for their familiars have been culled from their trial records.

Amie	Littleman
Besse	Makeshift
Collyn	Makhector
Elimanzer	Panu
Elva	Pigene
Fancy	Prettyman
Fillie	Priscill
George	Robert the Rule
Gibbe	Robin
Grissel	Rorie
Hoult	Rug
Inges	Sack and Sugar
Jacke	Sanders
Jarmara	Sathan
Jezebell	Sparrow
Lightfoot	Susan
	Tewhit
	Tibbe
	Tom
	Tyffin
	Vinegar Tom
	Wynowe

Animal Omens

When you see a frog in early spring, creep up behind it and gently stroke its back with your finger. You will know true love before the snow flies.

If you hear an owl hooting in the forest before midnight, it warns of trouble to come. If heard after midnight, it is a sign that death is near.

And if you see a spider:
in the morning — you'll know shame.
at midday — pleasure and profit.
in the afternoon — a gift it brings.
in the evening — joy and mirth.

Upon seeing crows, remember:
> *One for sorrow,*
> *Two for mirth,*
> *Three for a wedding,*
> *Four for a birth.*

It is a bad omen to meet or follow a flock of sheep.

Bad tidings in one quarter; an omen of disaster in another yet all witches know:
> *Black cat arrives,*
> *Good fortune thrives.*

A visit from a tricolored cat will bring good luck. If you can entreat it to stay, magic paths will open before you.

Should a black dog come to your home unbidden and take up residence with you — welcome the beast, for you can be sure good fortune will follow.

An Occult Bestiary

The interest in our kin of the animal world, which has existed since the dawn of time, developed into fables and cautionary tales of the Greeks and Romans. By medieval times a literary form known as the Bestiary was born. Combining lessons in natural history with Christian morals, the churchman used the popularity of beast-tales in an attempt to entertain as well as teach his doctrines.

Over the centuries, certain creatures of earth and air, as well as some that never existed at all, have become associated with mystery, magic and witchcraft.

THE LION

ITS MANE like tongues of fire, the golden lion is traditonally a beast of the sun. Probably because of its strength and size it was from earliest times associated with deities and royalty and as a symbolic guardian in stone still functions not only outside temples but libraries and palaces as well.

"The lion stands on a hill," wrote the anonymous author of a thirteenth-century English Bestiary. "If he hears a man hunting, or smells him through his nose, scenting his approach — by whatsoever way he wishes to go down into the valley, all his footprints he fill in after him. He drags dust with his tail wherever he steps — either dust or dew, so that the hunter cannot find him. Down he drives to his den where he will hide himself.

"Another trick he has. When he is newly born, the lion lies still; he stirs not out of his sleep until the sun has thrice shone about him. Then his father rouses him with the roaring that he makes.

"A third habit has the lion. When he lies down to sleep he will never lock the lids of his eyes."

THE UNICORN

"THERE ARE in India certain very swift white asses, their heads dark red, their eyes dark blue and in the middle of their forehead is a single spiralled horn which is about a foot and a half in length," so wrote the Greek historian Ctesias in *Indica*, the first mention of the mythological unicorn.

He goes on to describe the horn: its base "pure white, the middle portion is black and the tip is vivid crimson and very sharp," colors which Robert Graves explains are those of the triple-moon-goddess as described in Apuleius' *Golden Ass*.

Herodotus considered the unicorn as a genuine zoological specimen and may have seen a rhinoceros horn which seemed to prove it. Pliny in the first century A.D. wrote, "The fiercest animal is the unicorn, which in the rest of the body resembles a horse but in the head a stag with a single black horn three feet long projecting from the middle of the forehead. They say it is impossible to capture this animal alive."

Medieval legends, however, again echoing themes of the moon-goddess, provide an answer, "A virgin with gentle caresses and soft words can lull a unicorn to sleep. She must first be seated under a single tree in the forest alone before the unicorn will approach and lay its head in her lap."

Always a symbol of supreme power, vigor, and virility the unicorn has been associated with gods and kings. As a creature that represents a union of opposing principles, occultists link the beast with the androgynous Mercury.

THE HARE

THE HUMBLE hare has always been connected with witchcraft and has, according to folktales, often been the shape adopted by witches themselves. A spiritual symbol, for long it was sacred in Greece and the British Isles. In County Kerry, Ireland, a taboo about eating hares still exists. An ancient ban on hunting the hare, in fact, was lifted only once each year: on May Eve. Traditionally the penalty for hunting the hare at other times was to be struck with cowardice. The legendary British queen Boadicea carried a hare into battle against the Romans, letting it loose in the hope that the foe would strike at the animal with their swords and thus lose their courage.

Fishermen have invariably turned back if a hare crossed their path on the way to the sea, and even to speak its name was forbidden. Equally ancient are the hare's associations with fertility and the witch goddess Hecate.

THE PHOENIX

FROM the Near East in the land once known as Phoenicia comes the legend of the Phoenix, a once-in-many-lifetimes bird with glorious multi-colored plumage. The name, derived from the palm tree in which it reputedly dies and is reborn, may have been due to confusion on the part of the Greek travel writer Herodotus. On his visit to the Egyptian city of Heliopolis about 430 B.C., Herodotus reported:

"There is a sacred bird called the phoenix. I myself have never seen it but only pictures of it; for the bird comes but seldom into Egypt, once in every five hundred years, as the people of Heliopolis say. His plumage is partly golden and partly red, He is most like an eagle in shape and bigness. In a nest of myrrh and palm fronds he expires in flames ignited by the sun, From the ashes arises the successor."

Tacitus also mentions that the phoenix reappeared every five hundred years but adds that according to some estimates the figure is less, a sum amounting to four solar years plus one day. It is known that the Egyptians had no leap year and saved up the fragments and so the legendary journey of the phoenix from the place of sunrise to the chief sun temple at Heliopolis may well have celebrated the quadrennial event.

The phoenix, at any rate, stands for mortality and

immortality, the endless cycle of birth, death and new birth through which all life passes. Symbol of the sun and resurrection, prime mover of the world and prototype of the individual soul, the phoenix heralds a Great Year — the time required by the sun, moon and five planets to return to their initial positions. Thus upon the fulfillment of the vast astronomical cycle, history repeats itself, the phoenix mirroring the process.

Dragons

DRAGON legends capture the imagination in grand style. Having withstood the onslaught of scientific disbelief, dragon tales survive because the huge creatures are archetypes of fascinating and sometimes contradictory symbology and allegory.

It is not a simple matter to analyze the enigmatic dragon. Viewed as a manifestation of great power for aeons, the fabulous monster (often called serpent or worm in old texts) is undergoing a resurgence of interest today in England. This is doubtless in accord with the focus of attention on ancient British sites and traditions. The many qualities attributed to the dragon have led to a wealth of interpretations. Was the beast an actual creature, now extinct, to have been

feared or worshipped? Was it a symbol of protection, procreation, longevity, wisdom — or conversely: sin, temptation, savagery or death? The lore encompasses all these possibilities and more.

One source for the conception of the dragon may have been the discovery of bones or traces of gigantic primeval creatures, still said by some to exist in remote swamps and deep lakes. Another theory holds that "dragon" was a euphemism for England's invaders. Perhaps the tales were Christian fictions, propagated to teach a credulous peasantry about the relentless struggle between good and evil. In pre-Christian times and among certain esoteric sects after Christ's death, however, the dragon represented tran-

St. George slays the Dragon   Albrecht Dürer (1505)

scendental cosmic force. In heraldry it signified strength. Legends relate that King Arthur marched under a dragon banner. Many saints were renowned as dragon-slayers. The red dragon is the national symbol of Wales.

The Oriental dragon has always been a benevolent beast. Visual conceptions vary. The Chinese and Japanese dragons are scaly serpents, while the European equivalent is lizardlike and winged. Despite the difference in appearance and aspect, dragons universally share an association with water, caves, and hidden places where

treasure is concealed. Guarding secret wealth is the function most often performed by the dragon in legends and myths from all over the world.

The dragon image seems to have been coexistent with mankind's earliest realizations about the forces of nature and the cosmos. English dragons are specifically linked to many sacred sites of antiquity such as artificial mounds, geomantically shaped hills, wells, and ancient stone circles. The leys (terrestrial power lines) said to crisscross the British Isles are known as "dragon currents." It seems likely as scholars continue to investigate and assess the implications of ancient pagan shrines that dragon lore will assume new significance.

But the dragon is an elusive beast and not easily captured, even in the wispy net of our imagination. As archaeologist H. J. Massingham once wrote, "We may get all the dragons down to one dragon but there is no holding the lithe and weary heart and in a moment he slips through our hands."

Some Notorious Beasts

An excerpt from the *Folk-Lore Record*, published in England, 1878.

Durham — An ancestor of the Blackett family slew a monstrous reptile, dragon, worm, or flying serpent, in memory of which the descendants have to render service to the bishop at his first coming into the county by presenting him with a *falchion* (a sickle-shaped sword), and thereby secure to themselves the possession of a large estate.

— *Relics for the Curious*, 1824.

Essex — In the seventeenth year of Henry the Second, A.D. 1170, there was seen at St. Osythes a dragon of marvellous bigness, which by moving, burned houses

— *Baker's Chronicle*.

Gloucester — In the parish of Deerhurst, near Tewkesbury, a serpent of prodigious bigness was a great grievance to all the country by poisoning the inhabitants and killing their cattle. The king proclaimed that whoever killed the serpent should enjoy an estate in the parish which belonged to the Crown. One John Smith placed a quantity of milk in a place to which the serpent resorted, who gorged the whole agreeable to expectation, and then lay down to sleep. Smith then cut off its head with an axe. His family enjoyed the estate when Sir Robert Atkyns complled this account. Mr. Lane, who married a widow of the Smith family, had then the axe in his possession.

— *Relics for the Curious*, 1824.

Hereford — There is a tradition of a furious combat at Mordiford, near Hereford, between a winged serpent and a condemned malefactor, who was promised pardon on condition of his destroying the monster. He succeeded in killing the dragon, but fell a victim to the venom of his assailant's poisonous breath. A picture of the dragon was preserved in the church at Mordiford, and represents a flying serpent about twelve feet long, with a large head and open mouth.

— *Relics for the Curious*, 1824.

Oxon — Near Chipping Norton there was found in 1349, a serpent having two heads and faces like women, one being shaped after the new type of that time, the other after the manner of ancient attire, and it had great wings after the manner of a bat.

— *Stow's Annals*.

Sussex — At St. Leonard's Forest, near Horsham, there was seen in 1614, a strange and monstrous serpent or dragon, to the great annoyance and divers slaughters both of men and cattle. It was reported to be nine feet in length, a quantity of thickness about the middest, and somewhat smaller at both ends.

— *Harley's Miscellany*.

Yorkshire — At Wortley or Wantley, near Rotherham, there was a terrible dragon with wings, claws, teeth, and a sting in his tail, which was slain by a knight named More.

— *Percy Reliques*.

Some of the legends are said to be merely allegorical; thus the Mordiford dragon is set down as the flag of Uther, surnamed Pendragon, the chief of the Silures, about A.D. 448. And the Dragon of Wantley probably refers to Sir Francis Wortley, who, having bought a large estate, endeavored to acquire surrounding property by unfair means, in which he was resisted and defeated by a lawyer named More. Be this as it may, and these explanations are by no means universally admitted, the fact remains that there are many of these legends, and the belief in great land-serpents seems to have been general in old times. The most distinct, as well as the most recent, is the legend of the St. Leonard's serpent in 1614. This can possibly be traced to the Saurians, whose fossil remains are now found abundantly in the neighboring beds of Tilgate Forest. I believe there are few counties in England from which dragon legends, more or less definite, could not be collected.

— DRACO

Snakes and Rainbows

Snakes inspire more fear than esteem, and the dread goes beyond the fear of venom—most snakes are harmless. Death by snakebite is a rarity in America, but that doesn't lessen the mortal terror many people experience at the sudden sight of a wriggling snake. Jung pointed out that the snake represents the underworld and primordial matter, a prototype of the dark unknown, primitive, earthly, sinister. And the prevailing serpent myth of the Judaic-Christian world, its role as tempter in the Garden of Eden, accents its evil quality.

Yet some of us are instinctively drawn to snakes, fascinated by their subtle beauty, grace and swift, silent movement. Perhaps the snake lovers, long ago and in another incarnation, belonged to a culture that held the snake in high esteem and reverence. To the ancient Greeks and Romans the snake's habit of sloughing its skin symbolized renewal. Hermes/Mercury, the messenger god and spirit guide of the underworld, carried a snake-entwined staff, the caduceus. Asclepius, god of medicine, was also associated with snakes, and the caduceus be-

came the insignia of the medical profession. The sight of a serpent was regarded as an omen of healing to the ill, a certain promise of returning vigor.

The Gnostic sects in Alexandria around the turn of the Christian era chose a snake holding its tail in its mouth, the ouraboros, to depict the reconciliation of opposites. This Western version of the Oriental yin and yang, half in light and half in darkness denotes the potent phrase *en to*

pan, all is one. The drawing above is from a Greco-Egyptian text by a woman alchemist who chose the pen name Cleopatra. Her Chrysopeia (Gold-Making) was written in the third century A.D. and is preserved in a manuscript copy of the eleventh century.

Serpent worship turns up in a surprisingly wide variety of myths and legends. Ancient Egyptian deities and rulers are crowned with the sacred snake symbol, the uraeus. Voodoo venerates the serpent Damballah as the oldest and primary divinity, and snakes play a beneficent role in tales of the Australian aborigines and Native American tribes. The snake found its way into Toltec, Aztec and Mayan pantheons, emerging as the creator-god. Quetzalcoatl, the plumed serpent, was god of wind, wisdom and life. And although the snake often displays chthonic (underworld) aspects, it is also associated with rainbows linking heaven and earth.

Birds and Feathers

Fallen feathers of wild birds were once read as auguries. At moulting time in late summer, the wise would stroll into the countryside to collect as many as the eye could spy. Color was the important matter. A gray feather meant peace of mind, whether it fell from a nuthatch or a catbird. A black feather was a sign of death or disaster and probably added to the unfortunate reputation of the crow. The reading of the feathers could foretell the weather pattern ahead. A multitude of feathers foretold an early autumn, while a scarcity indicated a period of Indian Summer was at hand.

Feathers figure in many occult usages. A wreath of chicken feathers placed on the victim's bed warns of harm in the practice of Voodoo. The custom of sending a white feather to one who has betrayed a trust was observed in Victorian times. The exotic peacock feather bears ill will, the curse of the Evil Eye. Other feathers bring glad tidings. A red quill means good luck, and a blue one promises success in love. Present a traveler with a feather of good

will and his journey will be a pleasant one. The custom of securing a feather to a package sent by messenger is a charming old gesture, possibly one of the earliest forms of gift wrapping.

THE LANGUAGE OF FEATHERS

Red: *good fortune smiles upon you*
Orange: *a promise of delights to come*
Yellow: *beware of false friends*
Green: *adventure awaits*
Blue: *love will enliven your days*
Gray: *peace of mind*
Brown: *good health*
Black: *ill tidings or death*
Black and white: *disaster averted*
Green and black: *fame and fortune*
Brown and white: *joy and mirth*
Gray and white: *your wishes come true*
Blue, white and black: *a new love*
Purple: *exciting journey soon*

A Bevy of Swans

Many of England's earliest printed books dealt with the subject of hunting. It became customary to include in these volumes a listing of the proper terms designating groups of animals. The lists were called Nouns of Venery (an Old French word for the art of hunting) or Nouns of Assemblage. *The Book of St. Albans*, published in 1486, contained a considerable number of such terms. The following selection is drawn from that and other early sources.

Antelopes: a herd

Apes: a shrewdness

Asses: a pace

Badgers: a cete

Bears: a sloth

Bees: a swarm

Birds: a flock

Boars: a sounder

Bucks: a brace

Cats: a clowder

Cattle: a drove

Chickens: a brood

Cranes: a sedge

Crows: a murder

Cubs: a litter

Deer: a herd

Elks: a gang

Ferrets: a fesnyng

Fishes: a shoal

Flies: a swarm

Foxes: a skulk

Goats: a trip

Goldfinches: a charm

Hares: a down

Hawks: a cast

Horses: a harras

Hounds: a pack

Kangeroos: a troop

Kittens: a kindle

Larks: an exaltation

Leopards: a leap

Lions: a pride

Mares: a stud

Moles: a labor

Monkeys: a troop

Mules: a barren

Nightingales: a watch

Owls: a parliament

Peacocks: a muster

Ponies: a string

Porpoises: a school

Puppies: a litter

Ravens: an unkindness

Seals: a pod

Sheep: a flock

Squirrels: a dray

Starlings: a murmuration

Swallows: a flight

Swans: a bevy

Toads: a knot

Turtles: a bale

Whales: a gam

Wolves: a route

Woodpeckers: a descent

4 HERBAL SECRETS

Laurel

The tale of Apollo's amorous pursuit of the wood nymph Daphne (the Greek name for laurel tree) and her escape by transformation into a graceful tree inspired poets and painters. The disappointed god, in the words of the Roman poet Ovid, declared:

> Because thou canst my mistress be,
> I espouse thee for my tree:
> Be thou the prize of honor and renown;
> The deathless poet, and the poem, crown;
> Thou shalt the Roman festivals adorn,
> And, after poets, be by victors worn."

The bay or sweet laurel (*Laurus nobilis*) became a symbol of triumph in ancient Greece and Rome. The glossy green leaves woven into wreaths crowned poets and warriors. As protection against calamity, laurel trees were set before doors and in Rome guarded the gates of the Caesars. It was said that the emperor Tiberius always wore a laurel wreath during thunderstorms.

Oddly enough, while the myth tells of denied love, bay leaves figure in many love charms and amulets. A Greek maiden would burn dried laurel leaves with barley grain in an iron bowl wreathed with red wool at the time of the waxing moon to bring forth her lover, either lost or as yet unknown. Three bay leaves placed under the pillow will induce prophetic dreams. And bay leaves were chewed by the priestess at the Delphic oracle to enhance her prophetic inspiration.

Medieval sorcerers burned the dried leaves of the bay laurel tree to purify the atmosphere. Incense recipes often include one crumbled bay leaf to dispel negativity and evil. To bring forth flavor, bay leaves are used extensively in cooking today. The leaves, dried and packaged, are readily available on your grocer's shelves.

Vervain

A reader of magical texts is soon aware of the importance of vervain, which of all herbs is undoubtedly the most closely associated with medieval sorcery. The reputation of this herb stemmed from two sources — archaic European folklore and Roman literature.

During the early Middle Ages vervain was commonly used in spells and charms designed to erase heartache, longing, fear — any psychic burden. The name itself derives from two ancient Celtic words: *fer*, to take away, and *faen*, stone or weight. Throughout Europe in pre-Roman times, vervain was venerated and thought to possess remarkable powers. So mysterious were its qualities that

Apollo and Daphne   Ovid's *Metamorphoses* (1501)

the herb could only be gathered at night in that brief period before the new moon. Druidic priests of Devon and Cornwall used vervain for divination, inhaling the fumes of its incense. Along with St. John's wort and mugwort, vervain was traditionally tossed on the bonfires of Midsummer Eve celebrations.

Early American settlers brought vervain seeds to the new world. The alien plants escaped their gardens and today grow wild in forgotten meadows from Maine to Texas. At midsummer vervain reaches a height of about five feet, its slender green stems topped by spikes of tiny lavender blossoms.

Vervain's Latin name, *verbena*, means "sacred herb," and the plant was regarded as indispensable for purifying Jupiter's altar before the feast of that god. The herb was also associated with Venus and used in love charms. Roman ambassadors carried vervain as a kind of symbolic amulet and the herb was woven into garlands for certain religious festivals. The Roman poet Virgil makes reference to priests

> *In purest white...their heads attire,*
> *And o'er their linen hoods and shaded hair,*
> *Long twisted wreaths of sacred vervain wear.*

Virgil lived in the first century B.C. and achieved renown during the late Middle Ages not only for his poetry but for his magical skills. Perhaps his frequent mention of the sacred herb of witchcraft indicated his knowledge of the black arts, or so it seemed to medieval scholars. From Virgil's *Eclogues* (pastoral poems) the use of vervain as a love charm is noted: "Burn rich vervain and frankincense that I may array with magic spell to turn my lover's cold mood to passion!" Virgil wrote of vervain (along with cypress and yew) as a symbol of death. And there is a curious reference to vervain and death in a fourteenth-century grimoire (magical grammar) which recommends holding a sprig of vervain concealed in the palm when grasping the hand of a sick man. "Ask him how he fareth and how he hopeth of himself. If he feels he is doomed then he will die, but if he be hopeful of recovery,

so shall it be."

Vervain is one of the most versatile herbs in modern witchcraft. Its use as a love charm, amulet of protection, purifier preceding rituals, and as a means of relieving psychic distress all reflect the herb's ancient heritage.

St. John's Wort

The legendary powers of this bright yellow flowering herb date back at least as far as medieval times when it was believed to influence anyone opposing the will of a witch. Ignorant of its true use but aware of its power, the tormentors of witches held the plant to the mouths of those accused of malevolence to make them confess. It is interesting to speculate whether the presence of the sacred herb might have enabled a genuine witch to turn the tables and go free.

Originally called *Fuga Daemonum* (the flight of demons), the plant was accorded respect as providing protection against the force of evil thoughts. Irish folklore records the custom of carrying a bit of the herb under the left armpit as an amulet of protection.

People traditionally gather St. John's wort before sunrise on the day of Midsummer Eve. Any remaining dew on the petals was carefully collected in small vials to be used as an eye lotion through the coming year. That night, bundles of the herb were passed through the purifying smoke of the annual festival fires and bouquets were made to be hung above doors and windows to guard the home against the threat of fire, thunderbolts and other dangers. A maiden might place a sprig of the herb beneath her pillow and dream of a future love. And a childless wife, it was said, might end her barrenness if she would pick a spray of the plant while walking naked in her garden on Midsummer Eve.

The bright golden blossoms of St. John's wort resemble miniature suns and when infused in oil or alcohol change the color of the liquid to blood red. Similarly, if the petals are dropped in cold water, the water turns a golden hue. These properties and its curious balsamic odor

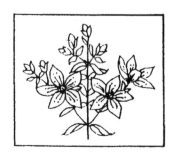

lend the plant an aura of mystery and many other customs and legends have grown up about it.

The most significant occult use of St. John's wort is only hinted at in printed books. The herb has the traditional power to protect witches. A bit of the plant worn on the person is said to have won the day in court judgements, business matters and in more personal contests of willpower.

In ancient times it was the custom upon Midsummer Eve (June 20) to build great fires and bid farewell to the sun as it began its annual retreat. From summer to winter solstice (June 21 to December 21), the daylight hours grow shorter and each day the sun appears to sink lower in the sky at noon. The coming of Christianity failed to eliminate the age-old fire festival but did manage to alter its date and change the name to celebrate the birthday of St. John the Baptist (June 24). That is why a sacred herb of witchcraft, Midsummer and the sun's retreat bears the name of a Christian saint.

Brewing Tisane

Every witch worthy of the craft can brew up a fine tisane. To serve the right herbal tea at the right time in the right way is a simple art, useful to all.

Bring fresh spring water to the boiling point. Add leaves to a scalded china or earthenware teapot. They may be fresh and whole or dried and crumbled. The amount of leaves and steeping time varies from plant to plant and is best determined by personal taste. Begin with a few leaves or teaspoonfuls to the cup. Pour in a small quantity of boiling water and cover the pot. Steep for a full minute. Add the remaining water, stir, cover, and steep for two more minutes. Strain and serve in fine porcelain cups, each of a different pattern.

Balm, lemon — one handful per cup, leaves are mild
Basil — cleanses and comforts, serve with honey

Bergamot — relieves nervous headaches
Catnip — soothes hysterics
Costmary — dried leaves are best, bitter if steeped too long
Goldenrod — cheers the spirits
Hyssop — excites passion
Lovage — pure pleasure
Mint — improves the digestion
Rosemary — helps expel morbid matter from the system
Sage — cures everything
Strawberry — leaves of the wild plant, a handful to a pint
Thyme — cures insomnia

The flavors of these green teas are usually subtle, and you will find that appreciation increases with experience. Milk and sugar are never added. Most tea herbs are available in the marketplace, including some made from flower heads such as red clover and mayweed. For the more adventurous, our colonial forebears thoughtfully stocked the eastern seaboard with their alien plants. Many in time escaped their gardens and now thrive along roadsides, in meadows and abandoned pastures, their ancient uses long forgotten. A fieldguide to wildflowers can help you identify these herbal treasures.

The Bath, Herbal and Ritual

By the flicker of candlelight, inhaling the fragrance of pungent incense, ease into a full tub of very warm herbal bath. You are about to give yourself over to an ancient ritual of cleanliness and purification. After scrubbing with a pure soap, close your eyes, relax your muscles section by section from head to toe. Focus your closed eyes at a point in the center of your forehead. Remain in the ritual bath from fifteen to twenty minutes.

You will emerge with your physical senses extended in a disciplined way, calm yet energized, with an increased subtle awareness of all about you.

The water may be prepared in a variety of ways. A sea salt bath is an ancient method for general tonic effect — add one pound iodized sea salt to the bath water. For a pine-needle bath, boil one pound pine needles and cones for a half hour, leave for thirteen hours to infuse, and strain. Use a gallon amount for each bath. Flowering herbs may be used, either prepared by infusion as for the pine-needle bath or tied in a cheesecloth bag and added to the bath water. Hyssop, camomile, lavender, bergamot, rosemary, thyme, and lemon verbena are traditional.

The Poison Plants

John Michell, in his *The View over Atlantis*, gives a highly evocative picture of a Druidic initiation ceremony:

Some potion was mixed as in the Cauldron of Keridwen, a brew of fruits, herbs and fungi, henbane, belladonna, aconite, the thorn apple and the spotted skin of the red birchwood mushroom, the various narcotics whose effects and seasons of potency were for long the study of native witches...The aspirant then descended into the bowels of the earth, perhaps into the passages of New Grange...or the catacombs below Glastonbury Tor. Those who survived the ordeal returned to the surface, and on the morning hilltop became inspired with wisdom and everlasting life.

I propose to take a closer look at the wonderfully illuminating plants of the ancients, known and loved by witches, magicians and sorcerers of all eras. There are mentioned in the passage above three plants of the nightshade family (*Solanaceae*), the most narcotic and hallucinogenic of all the plant families and, in immature hands, the deadliest. It is the group from which we get tobacco and the potato as well as the infamous mandrake, so it seems fitting to start with them.

Atropa belladonna

Common names: deadly nightshade, dwale, belladonna, devil's cherry, dwayberry.

A tall, stout, bushy perennial with broad, pointed oval leaves. It grows in waste places and among ruins, mainly on chalk or limestone in England. It is seldom found as a wildling in the United States. At the base of the leaves bloom solitary, large, dull purple flowers, bell-shaped and drooping. They blossom fom May to August and fruit a shiny black berry the size of a cherry.

The name *Belladonna* (beautiful lady) derived from the use of an extract of the berry's juice in the eyes by ladies during the Renaissance to enhance their beauty by creating a dilated doe-eyed expression much in vogue at that time. It was used by ancient Roman priests who drank an infusion of the plant's leaves before appealing to Bellona, goddess of war.

The active principle, atropine, first stimulates the nervous system and then paralyzes it, also causing muscular convulsions that must seem to a bystander like demons within wrestling for possession of the body. It also has a most powerful effect on the eyes, causing hallucinations, but may also involve headache, cramp, loss of appetite and mental stupor. The antidote for nightshade

DEADLY NIGHTSHADE — *Atropa belladonna*

poisoning is to be found, ironically, in the mushroom fly agaric (*Amanita muscaria*; see later), but the balance between the two is so delicate as to be a closely guarded secret.

Belladonna was used extensively in European witchcraft. It was said to be tended nightly by the devil himself except for Walpurgisnacht, when he departed to the mountains to prepare for the witches' sabbat, so that it could be collected with impunity on that night only.

Datura stramonium

Common names: thorn apple, stinkweed, Jamestown weed, jimsonweed, demon's herb, devil's trumpet

A distinctive, stout, hairless annual with an unpleasant smell; solitary, large, trumpet-shaped purple or white flowers; and a monstrous, spiny, chestnutlike fruit. An occasional weed or casual on waste or cultivated ground, flowering from June till first frost on both sides of the Atlantic.

The popular name jimsonweed, by which it is known to all who have any real knowledge of this herb, arose in 1676 when soldiers sent to Jamestown, Virginia, to quell a local rebellion unfortunately ate the plant. An eleven-day delirium followed, and the news of it spread throughout the colonies. The incident is described in Beverly's *History of Virginia*.

The active principle, hyoscyamine, is a drug similar to atropine but is twice as powerful in its effect on the peripheral nervous system. The effects of the *Datura* leaves are devastating. To start with, the body feels full of water. To move about requires immense concentration and usually ends up with the partaker falling by degrees, as if in slow motion, to the floor. There is a heightening of the senses, which is followed by a short sleep.

Upon awakening it seems as if one is transferred to a separate reality. Intense, vivid hallucinations flare up in front of the eyes; one sees objects and people that are not in the ordinary consensus reality. These hallucinations seem quite real, having substance both physical and mental, obeying no laws of the participant but moving and acting of their own volition. One also seems to be transported to other localities. Hallucinations occur and fall away to be replaced by others in an arbitrary but acceptable dreamlike sequence.

Various of the *Datura* species are used in the Americas. Carlos Castaneda has chronicled his use of *Datura inoxia* under the auspices of a Yaqui Indian called Juan Mateus in the book *The teachings of Don Juan: a Yaqui Way of Knowledge*. The book gives fairly detailed instructions about growing, preparing and using the plant. Don Juan used it for divination and in a "flying" ointment. The herb is also used in initiation ceremonies by South American Indian tribes.

HENBANE — *Hyoscyamus niger*

Hyoscyamus niger

Common names: henbane, hogbean, poison tobacco, henbell, Jupiter's bean

A stout, evil-looking and bad smelling biennial, with clammy, broad-toothed, unstalked leaves covered with sticky white hairs. Its flowers are a lurid creamy buff, purple at the base, with a network of purple veins. The calyx is green with five broad, stiff teeth, the tube swelling in fruit. Widespread but local in disturbed ground, flowering in England from June till August. It is found in the northeastern United States in waste ground of the older settlements, particularly in old gardens, cemeteries and ruins. The flowers may appear as early as May.

The active principle is hyoscyamine, from which the plant gets its scientific name. The action of the drug is described under *Datura*. The common name, henbane, is self-explanatory, bane meaning that which destroys life.

Henbane seems to have been the most popular of all the drug plants with European witches, probably because it is commoner than the thorn apple. It is reported to have been used in the conjuration of demons and the art of prophecy and was taken as a crushed powder of dried leaves in a drink. Most of the observations made for *Datura stramonium* would apply to this plant.

The leaves of one variety of *Hyoscyamus* are smoked in India and Africa for their inebriating effect, and henbane itself is included in a medieval recipe for a hallucinogenic incense.

JIMSONWEED — *Datura stramonium*

46

Because of the strength of the poisons in this herb it is very dangerous when used in excess over long periods, and the ancient sorcerers were agreed that excessive use could lead to madness.

Aconitum napellus

Common names: aconite, monkshood, wolf's-bane, blue rocket, friar's cap, Venus's chariot.

A beautiful, bright green, hairless, tall perennial, with spikes of helmeted blue violet flowers. Its natural habitat is mountainous regions, but it occurs as a garden escape in both England and America. Every part of the plant is deadly, especially the knotty black root. The flowers appear in July and August.

Its name, "monkshood," derives from the flowers, which resemble monks' cowls. An ancient tradition holds that wolves are partial to its roots and dig them out for winter food. Death follows swiftly; thus the name wolf's-bane. The plant is a member of the buttercup family (*Ranunculaceae*).

Ancient mythology calls aconite the deadliest of all poisons and attributes its invention to Hecate. The Chinese and the Celtic tribes of Gaul used it as an arrow poison. The famed physicians of Myddfai noted its value as a remedy in the *Meddgon Myddfai*, recorded in Wales in the twelfth century.

The active alkaloid, *Aconitum*, is a powerful poison, and the root contains about 0.4 percent, one-fifteenth of a grain of the alkaloid being a fatal dose. It has an action like an anesthetic, producing numbness when rubbed onto the body in an ointment. The drug appears to affect the sensory nerves but does not produce hallucinations. Its inclusion in the Druidic recipe seems to be due to its anesthetic properties.

Amanita muscaria

Common names: red birchwood mushroom, fly agaric, magic mushroom, divine mushroom, soma, haoma.

A brilliant yellow to deep red fungus common in Asia, Europe and America. It prefers poor soil and grows singly or in groups along roadsides, in groves of birch or pine trees and in marshes. Its cap is covered with white warts. White gills and a hollow stem differentiate it from the common mushroom.

Decoctions made from this mushroom are used to kill flies and have given it the name of fly agaric. It is, of course, world famous as soma and has been used by most races through all periods of history. It is the universal perch of fairies and is always shown in illustrations of children's stories and nursery rhymes. The various publications that deal with it are well known, so I shall give only a few facts here. Among the drugs so far isolated from the *Amanita* are:

Muscarine, which first causes vomiting and diarrhea, and later stimulates the parasympathetic nervous system so that the partaker is capable of great feats of strength and endurance.

Atropine, discussed under *Belladonna*.

Bufotenin, a secretion otherwise found in the skin of a toad, which lowers the pulse rate and temperature. A common name for the mushroom is, of course, the toadstool.

Amanita is unique in being inebriant both directly and in the urine of people who have ingested it. In the first form it can be taken as a fresh or dried cap; or by infusing the cap with hot water, beating the juices out and taking the juice with milk, curds, barley or honey; or mixed with the leaves of fireweed. The second method can be repeated several times with gradually lessening effect. In

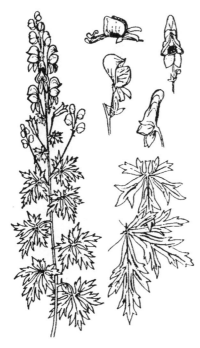

MONKSHOOD — *Aconitum napellus*

Siberia and Finland they drink the urine of a reindeer that has ingested the mushrooms. As game, the reindeer meat may provide inebriation. In Siberia the mushroom is preferred to Russian vodka, which is the only other form of liquor available. In Scotland, *Amanita* and whisky are taken together by poachers, this mixture being known a Cathie, supposedly in memory of Catherine of Russia, who fancied it.

After the *Amanita* has been consumed the participant falls into a light sleep in which fantastic and beautiful visual hallucinations pass in front of the eyes in a dreamlike sequence. In Russia the peasants claim to be visited by small red tubular beings who correspond in number to the mushrooms consumed and are supposed to be a kind of spiritual emanation of the eaten mushrooms. These beings can be engaged in conversation and often order the peasants to do all manner of dangerous, and sometimes fatal, actions. Often only the vigilance of sober friends pulls the participant back from the brink of disaster.

A shaman can use these little beings, with the correct form of questioning, to foretell future events and even lead the way to lost or stolen objects or to turn up buried treasure.

There is absolutely no mention of *Amanita* in any of the medieval grimoires that I have read. The fact that witches do use the plant was attested in a television program presented in England a few years ago that showed a witch with an *Amanita* on an altar.

These, then, are the Druidic plants. As can be appreciated, the potion from the Cauldron of Keridwen would have produced convulsions of the limbs and coma followed by the most inconceivable hallucinations. The amazing fact seems to be not that the initiates became inspired with wisdom and everlasting life but that any survived at all. This points to the excellence of the Druidic preparations. As a final thought, I cannot conceive of any better method for sorting out the wheat from the chaff. Any person who went into the initiation ceremony with the wrong motives, if not killed by the experience, would have been reduced to a gibbering idiot.

— NICHOLAS COURTNAGE

The Gundestrup Cauldron, a Celtic cult bowl of silver-plated copper measures three feet in diameter and is dated to the first century B.C. It was discovered in a peat bog in Gundestrup, Denmark in 1891 and now rests in the National Museum at Copenhagen.

Flying Ointment

Formulas for those trance-inducing ointments "whereby witches ride the aire" have been analyzed in recent years and found to contain in varying proportions the following ingredients: *Aconitum* (monkshood, wolf's bane), *Belladonna* (deadly nightshade), and *Cicuta virosa* (water hemlock, cowbane) combined with oil or fat. Not "the fat of young children" as claimed by the Christian demonologists in their effort to stamp out the witch cult. Hog's lard did as well and was a lot easier to obtain.

Reginald Scot in 1584 wrote of how witches "stamp all these together, and they rubbe all parts of their bodys exceedinglie, till they looke red, and be verie hot, so as the pores may be opened, and their flesh soluble and loose."

The herbs, deadly poison if taken orally, had a modified effect when rubbed upon the skin. The recorded effects of the unguents range from heightened awareness to visions of the future, and usually included tales of wild rides and revels.

A. J. Clark, in an appendix to Dr. Margaret Murray's *The Witch-Cult in Western Europe*, concludes that aconite in combination with belladonna might well have produced the sensation of flying by causing excitement and irregular heart action.

The Herb Gardener   Frankfurt (1562)

Planting an Herb Garden

An outdoor herb garden begins indoors, and your first gardening tools are pencil and paper. Planning at the very beginning will save you many later problems. Decide what specific herbs you really want and how large a garden they will require. As a general rule of green thumb, you can allow a circle with a radius of one foot around each plant. Some herbs require less and some more, but this is a convenient working average.

At this stage you will want to consider just how large a garden will be practical to handle. It is better to start out a bit on the small side; you can always expand gradually. Many novices tackle too much and later find that they have more than they can handle.

The most important step in planning the herb garden is choosing the site. The gardener must be concerned with two extremely important essentials, sunlight and soil. Most herbs require a great deal of direct sunlight, and starting an herb garden in a spot that is shaded half the day is courting disaster. If you live in the south or southwest, where sunlight is intense, you might get away with this kind of site. Otherwise don't plant in such an area unless you want to limit yourself to the shade-loving herbs such as the mints, sweet cicely, woodruff, and similar plants.

Most herbs also require a relatively light, limey, nourishing soil. If your soil is sandy, dig in some humus and possibly add some lime. Dolomite, an excellent form of lime, is relatively easy to handle. Eggshells and ground clam and oyster shells are less effective but of some value. With the heavy clay soil common along the eastern seaboard and in parts of the midwest, you will have to take more serious steps. If your site is well drained or on relatively high ground where drainage can be arranged, dig it up to a depth of two or three feet. Remove about half the spaded-up clay and replace it with a mixture of peat, builders' sand, and compost or humus. Gardeners near the seacoast have learned that seaweed is an excellent conditioner for heavy clay soils. Large quantities should be dug in, ideally in autumn so that the winter frosts can "work" the soil mixture. Seaweed that is well rinsed can be dug in during spring about a month before planting begins.

If the soil is acid or if you have spaded in a large quantity of peat, you will want to add lime in some form. Wood ash and some well-rotted manure will also help. Horse manure is better than cow manure, and rabbit manure is very good. Remember that any type of manure must be well-rotted before it is dug into the garden.

Drainage is an important factor. If your site is not well drained, there is little point in digging it up because a heavy rain will turn the garden into a huge mud puddle. Any gardener with a drainage problem would be wise to revive a medieval custom and raise the level of plant beds anywhere from a foot to two-and-a-half feet. In the Middle Ages the retaining walls of these beds were made of turf or wickerwork, and if you live in a damp climate you might consider turf. In a moist climate or with regular watering, the turf wall becomes attractively green and grassy — and turf is much cheaper than brick. However, you will have to clip the grass from time to time. If you prefer retaining walls of wood, brick or stone, make certain that the foundation goes below the frostline and that the walls contain numerous small drainage vents.

While your garden is still in the planning stage, work out groups of any plants with special needs. Decide where to put plants such as rosemary, thyme, and lavender, which require a somewhat sandy well-limed soil and a great deal of sun and air, and decide where to put the more acid and shade-loving herbs such as woodruff and angelica. It is best to isolate the mints (especially spearmint) as they tend to spread rapidly and crowd out their neighbors. Mugwort is another offender. Remember to place the shorter varieties in the front of the bed and the taller herbs like fennel, vervain, dill and comfrey in back.

In ancient times it was customary to make an offering and invoke the blessing of the Earth Mother when a garden was begun, and some traditionalists as well as many witches keep up this custom. The offering and invocations can take many different forms.

In some parts of the world the gardener walked around the spaded-up garden three times sunwise in a circle chanting a blessing, sometimes twirling a blazing torch, sometimes sprinkling water over all. When the first spadeful of earth was dug — or after the garden had been prepared but before the seeds were planted — an oatcake, cheese, and a glass of wine or ale were given to the Earth Mother in some special part of the garden. Another tradition, which probably goes back to the Neolithic period, calls for a libation of milk and an offering of honeycomb. And in Scotland and Ireland, three days before planting, the seeds were sprinkled with cold, clear spring water in the name of the gods. This was usually done on a Wednesday; the seeds were planted on a Friday, the day most auspicious for all operations not requiring the use of iron.

The contemporary herb gardener will probably prefer the modern method of planting seeds indoors in a sterile medium such as sphagnum moss and setting them out later to avoid "damp-off" and other hazards. But there is no reason why some of the old traditions could not be adapted to the sowing or the transplanting.

Once your garden is established and you have a regular schedule of watering and weeding, you should have few problems unless you are afflicted with rabbits, slugs, earwigs, or other pests. The only answer to rabbits, I fear, is a sturdy fence. Toads will usually eat the slugs, and earwigs can be attracted under inverted flowerpots during the day and then disposed of. Aphids may attack your basil and mint, but these pests are easily controlled by any number of organic sprays. Basil and nasturtiums are the most likely plants to be attacked by insects, and some people plant rows of nasturtiums to attract insects away from other plants. Most herbs are fairly tough, given the proper growth conditions in the first place.

If you live in a cold climate, cover your garden in winter with a thick mulch after the first frost and leave it until spring has definitely arrived. This will protect the plants from the dry, freezing winds of February and March, which can be fatal to the more tender herbs. From this point on, everything should be smooth sailing.

— J. WALTON FERGUSON

Herbs of Witchcraft

OF THE FIELD

Certain herbs acquire greater power under stress and seem to thrive in the garden no one tends — the wild. Those listed below are all alien plants, garden escapes, now masquerading as wildflowers or weeds. These ancient specimens perennially grace roadsides, railroad tracks, old meadows, vacant lots, swamps, woods, pine barrens and other waste places. You need only collect the smallest bouquets from most and a dozen or so leaves from the larger variety of herbs. Pleasant and rewarding, the quest is known from olden days as "wildcrafting."

Broom (*Cytisus scoparius*): A sprig of its yellow flowers in a soldier's cap lent courage in battle. The herb blooms in sandy soil from May through June. Wave a stalk in the air to raise a wind.

Clover (*Trifolium pratense*): Magic often favors a humble site and common clover is a case in point. Its three-leaf form is linked with the goddess Hecate. Called "trefoil" in old herbals that recommend its use in love charms. The plant blooms red-purple from May to September.

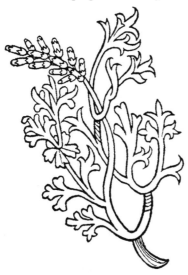

FUMITORY — *Fumaria officinalis*

Fumitory (*Fumaria officinalis*): The gray-green foliage looks like smoke rising from the earth, and smoke from burning dried and crumbled fumitory herb purifies an atmosphere for magical work. Rose flowers with purple tips bloom from May to August.

Mullein (*Verbascum thapsus*): From June to September many roadsides are brightened by the presence of the large yellow-flowered plant once called "The Hag's Taper." Collect its flannel-textured leaves to dry and beat to a

MULLEIN — *Verbascum thapsus*

powder. Use as a substitute for "graveyard dust," often required for certain spells.

Orpine (*Sedum telephium*): Orpine's folk name is "Midsummer Men." A maiden with romance on her mind was advised to collect a single pink blossom of orpine in silence and sleep with it beneath her pillow in order to dream of the man who would someday win her heart. The herb can be found during August and September in once-cultivated fields or along roadways.

St. John's wort (*Hypericum perforatum*): This sacred herb adorned with yellow flowers blooms from June to September. Its primary use in witchcraft is to strengthen willpower and protect its bearer from harm.

Tansy (*Tanacetum vulgare*): Its stalks are topped with bright golden buttons and its fernlike leaves emit a strong pleasant smell. The dried flowerheads and seeds wrapped in tissue paper guard treasured possessions. Tansy blooms from July to September.

Vervain (*Verbena officinalis*): The plant held sacred by the most diverse European cultures is quite modest to the eye. Its spikes of tiny lilac flowers with five petals comes to bloom from June to October.

Yarrow (*Achillea millefolium*): Yarrow is in evidence from June to August. A tight cluster of tiny dull white petals forms the flat flowerhead. Its aromatic leaves are fernlike. Yarrow is primarily a divinatory herb and often added to incense for that purpose. The dried, powdered flowers and leaves of the plant are part of many love charms.

IN THE GARDEN

Some herbal perennials prefer the shelter of a garden and yield best when tended with loving care. A witch plants leafy, above-ground crops while the moon is waxing to full. Seed sown from full to last quarter especially benefit perennials. The moon's place should be in one of the water signs — Cancer, Scorpio, Pisces. A moon in Libra is believed to favor flowering herbs. All the plants listed range between two to three feet tall with the exception of periwinkle, a creeping ground cover.

Hyssop (*Hyssopus officinalis*): Dark green leaves and blue, pink or white flowers add color to the herb garden. This highly aromatic herb is used in magic for purification and protection. It is easily grown from seed.

LAVENDER — *Lavandula officinalis*

Lavender (*Lavendula officinalis*): This is one of the nine herbs cast into the sacred fires of summer solstice eve. Its primary quality is fragrance and spikes of pale purple flowers are carried to attract the opposite sex.

Monkshood (*Aconitum napellus*): A deadly poison plant to be sure, but its beauty is beyond compare. Blue-purple flowers bloom from late summer to frost. Monkshood prefers shade and well-drained soil.

Mugwort (*Artemisia vulgaris*): Because of its invasive nature, some say mugwort deserves no place in the herb garden. But it may be wise to plant one clump by itself, for this is an herb with a myriad of mystic virtues. The dried leaves fill dream pillows. Carry a sprig on a journey to prevent fatigue. A wreath over the doorway protects the home from intruders.

Periwinkle (*Vinca minor*): This magic plant of shiny evergreen leaves and delicate pinwheels of lavender-blue flowers deserves its mystic reputation. Not only does it repel evil, it revives fading love and channels wayward thought.

Sage (*Salvia officinalis*): Burn dried sage leaves in the home to erase any lingering negativity after the departure of an unpleasant visitor or the receipt of a disappointing phone call. One of the most useful and satisfying garden plants, sage is strong and hardy. Cooks rely on its flavor.

Southernwood (*Artemisia abrotanum*): A unique herb that may become your favorite, for it offers a haunting scent and quiet shrublike beauty. While it receives little attention in old herbals or books about magic, southernwood blends well with many incenses, adding a curious element of surprise.

Tarragon (*Artemisia dracunculus*): The Latin name means "little dragon of Artemis," and the herb is believed to instill its wearer with the bravery attributed to the goddess of the hunt. Carry a sprig when you anticipate trouble. A handsome plant and a noble addition to any garden, tarragon is a treasure in the culinary art.

Wormwood (*Artemisia absinthium*): A proud plant of silvery leaves, wormwood contributes distinction to an herb garden. Associated with Mars and warriors as well as the Greek goddess of the hunt, wormwood guards against evil spirits. Burn its dried leaves to encourage clairvoyance.

FOR THE HOME

The indoor garden of a witch follows an old rule of keeping color, fragrance and magic alive during the dark season of winter. Along with bright geraniums for color, you may add the scent and magic of sacred herbs, for several will flourish as house plants.

ALOE — *Aloe vera*

Aloe (*Aloe vera*): A practical witch keeps an aloe plant close at hand in case of burns. Slit a frond to release the juice that immediately provides comfort and healing.

Catnip (*Nepeta cataria*): The herb is mainly grown for the pleasure it brings to cats. Long ago the minty plant acquired a reputation as a fertility charm. A tea made from its dried leaves restores confidence and eases the nerves.

GERMANDER — *Teucrium chamaedrys*

Germander (*Teucrium chamaedrys*): A lovely pine scent and the beauty of its dark green, glossy leaves and pale pink flowers recommend germander as an attractive pot plant. The French call it "little oak," for its form and leaves resemble that noble tree.

Jasmine (*Jasminum officinale*): This night-blooming plant has a natural association with love, for its scent is hauntingly lovely befitting that tender emotion. Scores of love charms employ the dried blossoms of jasmine, which look like tiny white trumpets ending in a star.

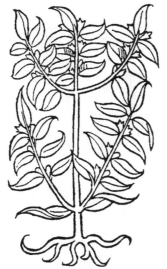

LAUREL — *Laurus nobilis*

Laurel (*Laurus nobilis*): Bay or sweet laurel is more a tree than an herb. As a tub plant, laurel may reach a height of four to six feet. Its old leaves fall only when new ones develop, so the tree is always green, a true emblem of immortality.

Myrtle (*Myrtus communis*): Herbal lore suggests myrtle is an emblem of love, fertility and marriage. A tub plant with a profusion of delicate bright green leaves and tiny white puff blossoms, a myrtle will grace any solarium. A myrtle bough symbolizes all new beginnings.

Rosemary (*Rosmarinus officinalis*): An essential herb in the indoor garden, with a great variety of magical virtues. The Latin name translates as "dew of the sea," and its gray-green needles of foliage and exquisite blue-lavender flowers appreciate moisture and a cool airy environment. Its scent increases mental agility and soothes loneliness. Rosemary is especially effective in love charms.

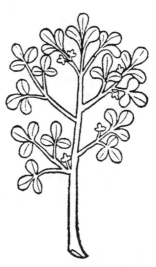

RUE — *Ruta graveolens*

Rue (*Ruta graveolens*): Rue is a protective herb that successfully drives away all evil spirits and intents. Its unique dark green leaves and unforgettable odor confirm the herb's potent quality.

Santolina (*Santolina chamaecyparissus*): You won't find this strange little plant mentioned in many herbals. Its coral-like form and silvery gray-green color marks santolina's individual nature. The Romans called it "ground cypress" and linked it to resurrection. Medieval lore declares santolina grants longevity. For unknown rhyme or reason, a current name for the herb is "Lavender Cotton."

Witch preparing a love charm   By an unknown Flemish Master, 15th century

5 CHARMS AND INCANTATIONS

In the beginning all arcane knowledge was transmitted orally. The novice witch learned by heart the chants, spells and rites required to perform an act of magic. As the world became literate, grimoires and books of shadows were born. Grimoires are books of ceremonial magic — texts produced during the Middle Ages. A book of shadows is the private journal of a witch. Adages, maxims, poetry and secret thoughts as well as the properties of sacred herbs, spells, incantations, charms, potions and philtres might be found handwritten in a typical book of shadows. No rule governs binding, number of pages, or contents. Each volume reflects the essence of its author.

Here are spells drawn from several books of shadows kept during the nineteenth and early twentieth centuries. In reciting an incantation, remember that the tempo should be far slower than that of ordinary speech. The desired effect is one of quiet emphasis and certain intent.

TO MAKE A WISH COME TRUE

With a thorn, prick the symbol of the waxing moon in a short, broad candle of pure beeswax. Light the candle and with eyes fixed upon its flame, concentrate on your wish as you chant:

Gracious Lady Moon,
Ever in my sight,
Kindly grant the boon
I ask of thee tonight

Blow out the flame but hold the memory of its light in your mind's eye for as long as you can. A way to make your wish come true will reveal itself.

TO MAKE LOVE GROW

Plant a flowerbulb in a clay pot that has never been used before. As you cover the bulb with earth, thrice repeat the name of the one you love. Then daily, morning and evening thereafter, say over it:

As this root grows
And as its blossom blows,
May my true love's heart be
Gently turned unto me.

TO IDENTIFY AN ENEMY

In a one-foot length of scarlet yarn, tie nine knots as you say:

These knots I knot
To know the thing, I know not yet,
That I may see
The one who is my enemy.

Sleep with the charm under your pillow and a vision of the person who means you harm will appear in a dream.

Bell, Book and Candle

Ring the bell, light the candle and open the book of shadows; a traditional preface to an act of magic. Later, this simple ceremony would become distorted into a Christian rite of exorcism. But in the early days, it belonged to the cult of the wise — the witches.

If you would learn to cast an enchantment or work a spell, remember the prime requisite is complete confidence in your ability to do so. The words and actions are mere formalities. The magic lies in the strength of your will and the power of your mind. These are fire charms and must be performed alone.

TO ATTRACT A LOVER

Crumble the dried leaves of the bay laurel tree and scatter them over live coals. As the leaves burn, firm your will and bring the face of your beloved to your mind's eye. Chant:

Laurel leaves,
Burn in fire,
Draw to me
My heart's desire.

TO RID ONESELF OF THE PAIN
OF UNREQUITED LOVE

Kneel before a roaring fire. As you hold a handful of dried vervain leaves, concentrate upon your intention. Throw the herb all at once on the blaze and repeat:

Here is my pain,
Take it and soar,
Depart from me now,
Offend me no more.

TO GAIN CONTROL OVER ANOTHER'S WILL

Take the dried leaves and flowers of St. John's wort, enough to make a generous handful. Strew them over the fire as you say aloud:

It's not the herb that I now burn,
But ....'s heart I mean to turn,
May he no peace nor comfort find,
Ere he bend to me in soul and mind.

Endearing Young Charms

Youth is a time of eager anticipation. We long to know what life holds in store for us and in particular, who will be our mate. Here are some very old charms used to foretell the future.

On the first appearance of the new moon after spring equinox, go out in the evening and stand in a meadow. Greet the descending crescent moon and say:

> *Haile to thee moon, all haile to thee;*
> *I prithee, dear lady, declare unto me,*
> *On this night, who my lover will be.*

Go soon to bed and in your dreams the face of your future beloved will be seen to smile and he will beckon to you.

This is an ancient Celtic charm chanted upon locating the constellations of Ursa Major and Ursa Minor — the Big and Little Dippers:

> *Great Bear, small bear,*
> *In the serpent winding;*
> *Hear now a simple prayer*
> *That love I may be finding*

The first person you meet the following day will lead you to your future love.

Gifts for the Making

Taking the time to make a gift is a tribute in itself. Gifting in witchcraft is traditionally a threefold process requiring a quest, a skill, and a spell. Here are three enchanting presents you can make for someone you love. These gifts will bring delight — and much, much more.

A WISHING BOX

The Quest — Find a tight-lidded wooden box that is small enough to hold in your hand. Attics, barns, antique shops, secondhand stores, garage sales, or even a swap-meet may provide the very box you seek. Let instinct guide your choice and don't settle until you've found exactly the right box.

The Skill — Lift the finish from the box with paint-remover if necessary and carefully sand away any surface roughness inside and out. If you're blessed with artitistic ability you might decorate the virgin wood with an occult design. If not, then merely apply stain to enhance the wood grain itself. Apply a protective coat of paste-wax to the outside surface and rub to a high finish. Line the interior (inside lid and base) with bright colored felt to match the personality of the recipient.

The Spell — Leaves of the bay laurel tree have potent magical power and have been used for thousands of years to bring forth a heart's desire. Boxes of dried bay leaves are easily obtainable in the herb section of supermarkets. Choose three whole leaves and place them inside the box. Let the box remain open in a harmonious atmosphere — one where kind words are spoken and tension is at a minimum — for the interval of a waxing moon. After moonrise each day hold the box aloft in your hand and as you raise it say:

> *Upon this box*
> *Let blessing fall,*
> *For......................,*
> *Its gifts enthrall.*

Using a wishing box: Write three wishes on three different colored papers. Fold each one over a bay leaf and place inside the box. The lid must remain closed until a wish comes true. Replace the granted wish with another.

THE WITCHES' LADDER

The Quest — You must collect nine different birds' feathers. This may sound difficult for a city dweller but sources are many: a zoo or park, a pet shop, or perhaps a friend with pet parrots. Other possibilities are the seashore, a country lane, chicken farm, or even your own backyard. Avoid the peacock's feathers and those of the black rooster; these have evil uses.

The Skill — Snip three-foot lengths from skeins of yarn in three different colors. Red, black, and white are often used but there is no hard and fast rule. Tie the strands firmly together at one end and braid them together into a cord as you say aloud:

> *Twist ye, twine ye, even so,*
> *Mingle threads of joy and woe.*

The word "woe" may give you pause, but this is a cord of life where sadness and joy both play a part. Knot the end of the braid. Now the nine feathers must be tied into the braid, one at a time, as you chant your progression. This requires patience and practice. You will find it easier if you make a loop first, insert a quill, and then pull the braided cord taut. During a trial run, try to keep your mind clear of thought until you're adept enough to secure the feathers at a steady pace.

The Spell — Concentrate with all your power upon the person for whom the gift is intended. Try to clearly visualize the happy fate you wish to provide. Don't let your mind wander as you perform this ritual.

> *Tie one, the spell's begun,*
> *Tie two, no power undo,*
> *Tie three, so shall it be,*
> *Tie four, forever more,*
> *Tie five, the charm's alive,*
> *Tie six, its magic fix,*
> *Tie seven, now under heaven,*
> *Tie eight, work winds of fate,*
> *Tie nine, to my design.*

Secure the ends of the cord together to form a circle.

This ancient charm may be made for good or ill. Italian witches call it *la guirlanda delle streghe* — "the

witches' garland," and in Voodoo a feather wreath is considered one of the most powerful *bakas* or magical talismans. Whoever receives the witches' ladder is advised to hang it high in a room where carefree time is spent. Its magic can be undone only by the witch who tied it.

A WITCHES' BOTTLE

The Quest — A small amount of mercury (quicksilver) is the heart of this charm. An old thermostat or thermometer might supply your need, or check the chemical supply houses listed in your telephone directory. A difficulty may be that the smallest amount they will sell is far more than you require and very expensive as well. Mercury is a fascinating element and a dangerous one. Handle with care.

You will need three glass containers with lids to fit neatly one into another. A survey of your medicine chest, refrigerator, or kitchen cabinet should solve this part of the quest. Make a collection of beautiful pebbles and/or small seashells and a good quantity of sand.

The Skill — Transfer the mercury by medicine dropper to a tiny bottle or vial. Make certain the cap is tightly closed. Fill the second glass vessel with water from the sea or a swiftly moving brook. Drop the vial with the mercury into it and screw the lid on tight. The third jar should be quite a bit larger, for it must hold the pebbles, shells, and a good quantity of sand. Fill to three-quarters with the stones and shells; make a well in the center to allow the sand to cradle the water jar and hold it upright. Carefully arrange the units so that the interior jars of water and mercury are hidden from view. The lid of the master jar can be decorated in any way you choose — this final touch belongs to your imagination and inventiveness.

The Spell — A witches' bottle protects its owner from harm and as such, is a splendid housewarming present. While you seek and assemble the ingredients of this charm, keep the idea of protection in your mind. Just before presenting it, place the jar on a table and with your major hand (the one you write with) make three circles in the air above the gift as you say:

> *Earth holds water,*
> *Water holds life,*
> *Life in safekeeping,*
> *Free from all strife.*

Departure for the Sabbat   Hans Baldung (1514)

6 MAGICAL SYSTEMS

Magic Circles

> *Draw a magic circle*
> *And sign it with a dot.*

You may recall this chant from childhood. It describes one of mankind's oldest symbols, so old that its origins are lost in antiquity. The circle around a dot has in various times and places represented the sun or the air. The

same symbol also stands for the unborn child — the dot an innermost essence protected by the circle or enfolding body. It is a short step from this concept to an understanding of the Wiccan Rounde — a hallowed space created for worship. Down through the centuries comes this directive:

"Now all join hands to form a ring surrounding the Baal (leader). Heads turn left and eyes tightly shut as a flowing force of thought is conceived, moving from one through the next and on, gathering strength as it goes — without beginning or end. When the circle is set thus, in motionless intensity, the Baal begins to clap to the rhythm of the heart beat. And upon this signal, all eyes open. Those joined side-step widdershins (against the sun's course)... slowly at first as in a formal dance, now gaining speed to respond to the quickened beat until three rounds are com-

Magic Circle for Evocation from Francis Barrett's *The Magus*

Agrippa's *Great Circle* from his *Occult Philosophy*

plete. This must be accomplished smoothly and without awkwardness. The space within the circle is now sanctified and the ritual work may begin."

The term "Baal" in this context was probably written down from an oral rendition and has no connection with the god Baal or the Phoenician word for "lord." It seems more likely that a link exists with the Celtic prefix meaning "bright" or "shining" as in Belenus, a Celtic fire god, and Beltane, the Celtic name for the May Eve festival (Roodmas) where bonfires are traditional.

While the witches' circle sanctifies, the ceremonial magician's circle protects. According to *The Key of Solomon*, the circle must be nine feet in diameter and drawn with an athame, or sacred knife. In manuscripts preserved at the Bibliotheque de l'Arsenal in Paris, one can find a variety of circle designs to suit any purpose from calling up demons to finding buried treasure. The prevalence of Hebraic symbols within these circles indicate the strong Cabalistic influence.

The casting of the circle is a feature retained by most forms of modern witchcraft. Many groups adhere to a diameter of nine feet as directed by ritual magic but the circle may be drawn in chalk or defined by boughs of greenery rather than marked by an athame. Two outer circles at six inch intervals, or an inner one of eight feet, may be added depending on the ceremony to be performed. As each coven is autonomous, no hard or fast rule governs ritual. Many in the craft simply join hands to form a ring. Each of these methods achieves its purpose.

Names

Names are magic. A change of name is often a deciding factor between success and failure. A new personality of unsuspected verve and assurance may emerge when it is provided with its true name.

Perhaps your given name is a source of vague uneasiness to you. It is rather as if in a former life you bore another with which you feel strongly identified. Some, in a lightning flash of déjà vu, are fortunate enough to recall that name. Others continue to know the elusive feeling that the name they bear is not their own.

Here is a list of common given names from a century ago. We include their language source and original meaning. Perhaps one will awaken a slumbering memory.

A

Abigail (Hebrew) Daughter of joy.
Adelaide (Teutonic) Of noble rank.
Adolf (Teutonic) Noble wolf.
Agatha (Greek) Good; kind.
Agnes (Greek) Chaste; pure.
Albert (Teutonic) Nobly illustrious.
Alden (Anglo-Saxon) Old friend.
Alexander (Greek) A defender of men.
Alexis (Greek) Help.
Alfred (Anglo-Saxon) Elf in council.
Alicia (Greek) Truth.
Amanda (Latin) Worthy to be loved.
Ambrose (Greek) Immortal; divine.
Amy (Latin) Beloved.
Andrew (Greek) Strong; manly.
Anne (Hebrew) Grace.
Archibald (Teutonic) Nobly bold.
Arnold (Teutonic) Strong as an eagle.
Arthur (Welsh) Healer.
Aubrey (Teutonic) Elf ruler.
Augustus (Latin) Majestic.
Avis (Latin) Bird.

B

Baldwin (Teutonic) Courageous friend.
Barbara (Greek) Foreign; strange.
Bartholomew (Aramaic) Warlike son.
Basil (Greek) Kingly; royal.
Beatrice (Latin) Making happy.
Benedict (Latin) Blessed.
Bernard (Teutonic) Bold as a bear.
Bertha (Teutonic) Bright.
Bertram (Teutonic) Bright raven.
Blanche (Teutonic) White.

Bridget (Irish) Strength.
Bruno (Teutonic) Brown.

C

Caleb (Hebrew) Dog.
Camilla (Latin) Attendant at a sacrifice.
Candida (Latin) Shining white.
Carmen (Spanish) Song.

Cecil (Latin) Dim-sighted.
Charissa (Greek) Grace.
Charles (Teutonic) Strong; manly.
Christopher (Greek) Christ-bearer.
Clara (Latin) Illustrious; bright.
Claude (Latin) Lame.
Clement (Latin) Mild; merciful.
Conrad (Teutonic) Bold counselor.
Constance (Latin) Firmness.
Consuelo (Spanish) Consolation.
Corinna (Greek) Maiden.
Curtis (Old French) Courteous.
Cyril (Greek) Lordly.

D

Daniel (Hebrew) God is my judge.
Daphne (Greek) Laurel.
Darius (Persian) Possessing wealth.
David (Hebrew) Beloved.
Deborah (Hebrew) A bee.
Dexter (Latin) On the right hand.
Diana (Latin) For the goddess.
Dolores (Spanish) Sorrows.
Dominic (Latin) Belonging to the lord.
Donald (Gaelic) World ruler.
Dorcas (Greek) A gazelle.
Dorothy (Greek) Gift of god.
Dulcie (Latin) Charming; dear.
Duncan (Gaelic) Brown warrior.

E

Earl (Anglo-Saxon) Man; noble.
Edith (Anglo-Saxon) Pleasure.
Edna (Hebrew) Rejuvenation.
Edward (Anglo-Saxon) Guardian of property.
Eli (Hebrew) High.
Elizabeth (Hebrew) Worshipper of God.
Elmer (Anglo-Saxon) Noble and famous.
Elva (Teutonic) Elf.
Enoch (Hebrew) Dedicated.
Ethan (Hebrew) Firmness; strength.
Ethel (Anglo-Saxon) Noble.
Eudora (Greek) Generous.

Eunice (Latin) Happy victory.
Eve (Hebrew) Life.
Ezra (Hebrew) Help.

F

Felicia (Latin) Happiness.
Felix (Latin) Happy; prosperous.
Fiona (Celtic) White.
Florence (Latin) Prosperity; bloom.
Francis (Teutonic) Free.
Franklin (Middle-English) A freeman.
Frederick (Teutonic) Good counselor.
Frieda (Germanic) Peace.

G

Gabriel (Hebrew) Man of God.
George (Greek) A husbandman.
Gerald (Teutonic) Spear wielder.
Gideon (Hebrew) A feller of trees.
Gilbert (Teutonic) Bright wish.
Giles (Old French) A kid.
Godfrey (Teutonic) Peace of God.
Grace (Latin) Favor.
Gregory (Greek) Vigilant.
Guy (Teutonic) A leader.

H

Harold (Anglo-Saxon) Army leader.
Hedda (Germanic) War.
Hedwig (Germanic) Strife.
Helga (Teutonic) Holy.
Henry (Teutonic) Chief of a house.
Herbert (Teutonic) Glory of the army.
Herman (Teutonic) A warrior.
Hepzibah (Hebrew) My delight.
Hilary (Latin) Cheerful; merry.
Hilda (Anglo-Saxon) Battle maiden.
Hiram (Phoenician) Most noble.
Honora (Latin) Honorable.
Hortense (French) A lady gardener.
Hugh (Teutonic) Mind.
Hugo (Latin) Spirit; soul.

I

Ira (Hebrew) Watchful.
Iris (Greek) Rainbow.
Isadora (Greek) Gift of Isis.
Isaac (Hebrew) Laughter.

J

Jason (Greek) A healer.
Jeremiah (Hebrew) Exalted of the Lord.
Jerome (Greek) Bearing a holy name.
John (Hebrew) God is gracious.
Jonah (Hebrew) A dove.
Jonathan (Hebrew) God has given.
Joseph (Hebrew) He shall add.
Joshua (Hebrew) God of salvation.

Judith (Hebrew) Praised.
Julius (Greek) Soft-haired.
Justin (Latin) Just.

K

Kenneth (Gaelic) A leader; commander.
Kore (Greek) For the goddess.

L

Lars (Etruscan) Lord.
Laura (Latin) Laurel.
Leila (Aramaic) Dark as night.
Leo (Latin) Lion.
Leonard (Greek) Strong as a lion.
Leopold (Teutonic) Bold for the people.
Leroy (Old French) Royal.
Letitia (Latin) Happiness.
Linda (Spanish) Lovely.
Linus (Greek) Flaxen-haired.
Louis (Teutonic) Famous warrior.
Lovell (Old English) Beloved.
Lucius (Latin) Light.
Luther (Germanic) Illustrious warrior.
Lydia (Greek) Native of Lydia.

M

Malcolm (Gaelic) Servant of Columba.
Margaret (Greek) A pearl.
Martha (Aramaic) Lady; mistress.
Martin (Latin) Warlike.
Marvin (Teutonic) Sea friend.
Matilda (Teutonic) Mighty battle maid.
Matthew (Hebrew) Gift of Jehovah.
Maurice (Latin) Moorish; dark-colored.
Melanie (Greek) Black.
Melissa (Greek) Bee.
Mercedes (Spanish) Mercies.
Michael (Hebrew) Who is like God?
Miranda (Latin) Admirable.
Morgan (Welsh) A dweller on the sea.
Murdoch (Celtic) Sea man.

N

Nadine (French-Russian) Hope.
Naomi (Hebrew) My sweetness.
Nathan (Hebrew) Gift.
Neil (Gaelic) Courageous.
Nicholas (Greek) Of a victorious army.
Noah (Hebrew) Rest; comfort.
Norman (Scandinavian) Norse man.

O

Octavia (Latin) The eighth born.
Olivia (Latin) An olive.
Oscar (Gaelic) Bounding warrior.
Oswald (Anglo-Saxon) Power of God.

P

Patrick (Latin) Noble; a patrician.

Paul (Latin) Little.
Penelope (Greek) A weaver.
Perry (Anglo-Saxon) Pear tree.
Philip (Greek) A lover of horses.
Phoebe (Greek) Shining.
Phyllis (Greek) A green bough.

Q

Quentin (Latin) The fifth born.

R

Rachel (Hebrew) A ewe.
Raphael (Hebrew) God hath healed.
Raymond (Teutonic) Wise protection.
Regina (Latin) Queen.
Reuben (Hebrew) Behold, a son!
Rhoda (Greek) A rose.
Richard (Teutonic) Strong ruler.
Robert (Teutonic) Bright in fame.
Roderick (Teutonic) Rich in fame.
Roger (Teutonic) Famous with the spear.
Roland (Teutonic) Fame of the land.
Ronald (Old Norse) Strong ruler.
Rufus (Latin) Red-haired.

S

Sabrina (Latin) A Sabine woman.
Salome (Hebrew) Peace.
Samuel (Hebrew) His name is El.
Sarah (Hebrew) A princess.
Seth (Hebrew) Appointed.
Sibyl (Greek) Prophetess.
Silvester (Latin) Rustic.
Sophia (Greek) Wisdom.
Stella (Latin) Star.

Stephen (Greek) Crown.
Susan (Hebrew) A lily.

T

Tabitha (Aramaic) A gazelle.
Thalia (Greek) Blooming; luxuriant.
Thea (Greek) Goddess.
Theodore (Greek) Gift of gods.
Thomas (Hebrew) A twin.
Thirza (Hebrew) Pleasantness.
Thurston (Scandinavian) Thor's stone.
Timothy (Greek) Honoring gods.
Tobias (Hebrew) The Lord is my good.

U

Ulysses (Greek) A hater.
Una (Latin) One.
Urania (Greek) Heavenly.
Urban (Latin) Of the city; courteous.
Ursula (Latin) She-bear.

V

Valentine (Latin) Strong; powerful.
Vera (Latin) True.
Victoria (Latin) Victory.
Vincent (Latin) Conquering.
Vivian (Old French) Full of life.

W

Walter (Teutonic) Ruling the host.
Wilfred (Teutonic) Desirous of peace.
William (Teutonic) Resolute helmet.
Winifred (Anglo-Saxon) Win-peace.

Z

Zachary (Hebrew) Remembered of Jehovah.
Zadok (Hebrew) Just.

AN OCCULT
Glossary

ADEPT — A skilled practitioner of the occult arts.

ALCHEMY — Medieval science dedicated to turning base metals into gold.

AMULET — A charm worn to avert evil and attract good luck.

ARADIA — The legendary daughter of deities Diana and Lucifer, destined to teach witchcraft to mortals.

ARCANE — Descriptive word meaning secret knowledge of the ancients.

ARCHETYPE — The original model or pattern.

ASTRAL BODY — Spirit body.

ATAVISM — Of or pertaining to a remote ancestor in instinctive memory.

ATHAME — Black-hilted knife used in the rites of a ceremonial magician.

AUGURY — Divination.

AURA — A halo or emanation of light surrounding an individual.

AVALON — The Celtic abode of the blessed; paradise of Arthurian legend.

BALEFIRE — A great fire blazing in the open air; a bonfire.

BANE — That which destroys life.

BANSHEE — Gaelic spirit whose wail warns of approaching death.

BARD — Celtic poet; a singer of tales.

BELTANE — Celtic name for the festival celebrated on May Eve.

BLOCULA — An Elfdale county estate where Swedish witches attended the sabbat festivals.

BLOODSTONE — A green gem sprinkled with red spots; the heliotrope of magic.

BOOK OF SHADOWS — A collection of ancient rituals, chants, spells and enchantments copied down in the hand-writing of a witch.

BRIDE — Brigit, Bridget, or Brid is the pre-Celtic goddess of Ireland symbolizing the promise of spring.

BROCKEN — The highest peak in the Hartz mountains of northern Germany known as a gathering place for witches.

BY KYNDE — By nature, or instinct.

CABALA — Hebraic system of mystical thought; an esoteric doctrine of urban medieval society.

CERNUNNOS — Pagan horned god of western Europe; stag-god of Gaul.

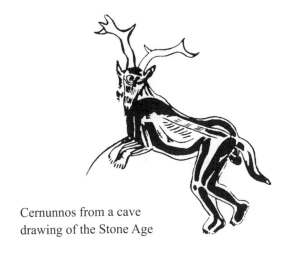

Cernunnos from a cave
drawing of the Stone Age

CANDLEMAS — A festival of light observed on the eve of February 2. Also the Feast of Bride that celebrates the coming of spring.

CHALICE — A silver cup used in sacred ceremonies of witchcraft.

CHANGELING — A child secretly exchanged for another in infancy.

CONE OF POWER — The collected force of powerful wills focused on a single purpose.

COVEN — A group of witches working to achieve a common purpose.

CULT — A shared system of belief or worship.

CUNNING MAN — Known in Elizabethan England as one thought able to combat the will of witches.

DEASIL — To move sunwise or clockwise, from left to right. A charm performed by going three times around an object carrying fire in the right hand.

DEJA VU — Fleeting personal memory of a previous life.

DEMETER — Greek goddess of the earth; known to the Romans as Ceres.

Diana as Goddess of the Hunt

DIANA — Roman goddess of the Moon and the hunt; called Artemis by the Greeks.

DIONYSIAN MYSTERIES — Rites of worship celebrated to honor the god of the vine and earth.

DRUID — One of the priestly class of Celtic culture. A modern follower of ancient ways.

DUALISM — A philosophical concept of opposing principles which form the ultimate nature of the universe as, for example, good and evil.

DYAD — Two units; a pair.

ELEUSINIAN MYSTERIES — Rites dedicated to the worship of Demeter and Persephone.

EQUINOX — The time when day and night are of equal length.

FAMILIAR — Animal helper of a witch in casting enchantments and working spells.

FETCH — Apparition.

FETISH — An object possessing magic power derived from the spirit dwelling within it.

FREYA — Nordic goddess of love for whom Friday is named.

Freya's chariot is drawn by cats

GNOSTICISM — The system of philosophy and religion which asserts mankind may possess inner knowledge by direct revelation.

GRIMOIRE — A text of magical rites and spells.

HALLOWMAS — November Eve festival of witchcraft.

HECATE — Patroness of witchcraft; a triple goddess of the Moon, Earth, and Underworld.

HERODIAS — Goddess of witches; Diana as Queen of the Night.

HEX — A spell or a charm, derived from the German word for witchcraft.

HIEROPHANT — High priest of the Greek Eleusinian Mysteries.

HUBRIS — Man's exasperation with fate and life's limitations.

I CHING — Chinese Book of Changes; collected wisdom of ancient origin.

INCANTATION — Chant spoken slowly with a strong and firm intention.

JANUS — Double-faced Roman god who watched both the rising and setting Sun.

LA TENE — The Iron Age in Europe, dating from 800 B.C. to A.D. 100.

LAMMAS — Festival of witchcraft held on August Eve to insure good harvest.

LIGATURE — A binding.

LOKI — Nordic god of fire.

LUGHNASSAD — Celtic name for the August Eve celebration.

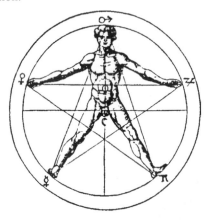

Man as Microcosmos from Agrippa's *Occult Philosophy*

MACROCOSM / MICROCOSM — The universe as contrasted to man; what is equal above, is equal below.

MAGUS — Wise man.

NEED-FIRE — A flame produced by friction in ceremony used to ignite the bonfires of May Eve.

ODIN — Nordic god of wisdom and poetry. Also called Woden.

OIMELC — Celtic name for the celebration held on the eve of February 2.

OVERLOOK — To cast a glance of power for good or ill.

OWL TIME — Between midnight and one o'clock; the 13th hour.

PENTACLE — Five-pointed star, an ancient symbol of perfection used from the time of Pythagoras, Greek philosopher and mathematician, 6th century B.C.

PERSEPHONE — The daughter of Demeter / Ceres who was abducted by the god of the underworld. Her return each year symbolizes springtime. The Romans called her Proserpine.

The Abduction of Persephone

PHILTRE — A potion prepared to produce a magical effect, especially a love charm.

PSYCHE — The human soul, the mind, the inner thought.

RITES OF PASSAGE — Human transitions celebrated at birth, puberty, marriage and death.

ROODMAS — Anglo-Saxon name for the May Eve festival.

RUNES — Germanic alphabet derived in large measure from the Greek and Roman; formed with straight lines to facilitate carving on stone and wood.

SABBAT — Feast. Major sabbats are November Eve, February 1, May Eve, and August Eve. The lesser sabbats are celebrated at winter and summer solstices; spring (vernal) and autumnal equinoxes.

SAMHAIN — The Celtic name for the sacred November Eve celebration; Hallowmas.

SATANISM — Christian devil worship; an inversion or parody of Christian faith.

SCRY — To divine by means of crystal ball, mirror or other reflective surface.

SHAMAN — Sorcerer of primitive tribes. A medium between the visible and the spirit world.

SIGNATURES, DOCTRINE OF — The belief that each plant bears a visible key to its use.

SOLITARY — One who practices the art of witchcraft alone.

SOLSTICE — The longest day of the year, Midsummer Day, June 21; the shortest day, December 21, when the

Sun begins its return and the days lengthen.

SOOTH — Truth.

SWAN-ROAD — The sea.

TALISMAN — An object marked under certain conditions of the heavens to act as a charm against evil.

TRADITIONALS — A term used to designate members of the witch-cult who practice rites handed down through the generations; hereditary witches.

VATES — Prophets.

WALPURGISNACHT — Germanic name for the May Eve festival.

WATCHERS — The sleepless ones or "fallen angels" of Hebrew legend who mated with the daughters of men to whom they taught the forbidden arts.

WARLOCK — An Anglo-Saxon term of derision, i.e., a liar and betrayer of trust.

WIDDERSHINS — Backward, or in a direction contrary to the apparent motion of the Sun. To move counter-clockwise.

WITCH — From the Anglo-Saxon "wiccan" or wise. One blessed with supernatural gifts.

WITCH BALLS — Spheres of colored glass intended to thwart evil spirits and protect the home.

WORT — Any plant or herb.

WYRD — Anglo-Saxon goddess of destiny.

YULE — Norse feast celebrating winter solstice.

ZOROASTER — Prophet who flourished in Persia about 1000 B.C.

Rune Magic

Runes are secret signs used extensively by Teutonic peoples from as early as the beginning of the Christian era. In rune magic the symbol actually becomes the object or thought after which it is named, and with it good and evil can be worked. The mystical properties of each rune were known only to the shaman of the tribe in ancient times. Christian ordinances were issued against the practice of rune magic; thus only a few of archaic significance have come down to the present.

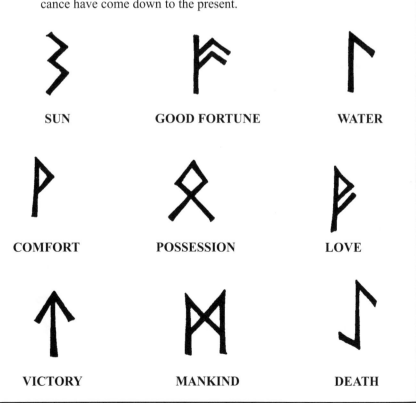

SUN	**GOOD FORTUNE**	**WATER**
COMFORT	**POSSESSION**	**LOVE**
VICTORY	**MANKIND**	**DEATH**

AN OCCULT
Alphabet

In 1801 Francis Barrett, English scholar of occult philosophy and the Cabala, published a curious volume called *The Magus.* Among the illustrations we find this occult alphabet. Its legend reads, "The Mysterious Characters of Letters deliver'd by Honorius call'd the Theban Alphabet." Honorius II, Pope from 1216 to 1227, sponsored a crusade to Egypt and was reputed to

be a master magician. Several medieval *grimoires* (magical texts) are attributed to him.

Our English J, U and W had no equivalents in Middle Latin. Modern occultists use the symbols for I and V as substitutes for the missing letters. The final character has been translated as the Greek *alpha* and *omega,* the beginning and end.

Names and Numbers

Two major systems are used to turn names into numbers. We prefer the one developed by the sixteenth-century adept Agrippa and used by the famed Cagliostro in the 1700's. Based upon the Hebrew alphabet, it accords each letter the following numerical value.

A — 1	E — 5	I — 1	M — 4	Q — 1	U/V — 6
B — 2	F — 8	J — 1	N — 5	R — 2	W/X — 6
C — 3	G — 3	K — 2	O — 7	S — 3	Y — 1
D — 4	H — 5	L — 3	P — 8	T — 4	Z — 7

To find your number, write your name. Beneath each letter, record its equivalent number. Add these figures together. If your total has two or more digits add them, and repeat until you reach a single number. As an example:

```
S  Y  B  I  L    L  E  E  K
3  1  2  1  3    3  5  5  2    equals 25. And 2 + 5 = 7
```

Each number has a significance. Positive and negative values are as follows:

1

Independent, powerful, and original in thought. Coldly aggressive; often ruthless.

2

Gentle, thoughtful, and of a kindly nature. Easily thwarted and thus capable of guile and deceit.

3

Brilliant, spirited, and light of heart. Blessed with talent and luck but often careless of both. Unduly concerned with the opinions of others.

4

Calm, dependable, hard workers. Lacking creativity and originality, they resent change. A capacity for both wild rage and melancholia exist.

5

Exciting, energetic, but restless spirits. They often court danger for its own sake. A certain irresponsibility mars their charm.

6

Reliable, tactful, home-loving souls. A genuine gift for creating harmony may be flawed by an undue attention to detail and trivia.

7

Mystics of powerful and well-disciplined intellect. Aloof, impatient of stupidity; sarcastic and deeply resentful of criticism.

8

Tough, able, and most successful in dealing with practical matters. A tenacious stubbornness can extend to tyranny.

9

Romantic, idealistic humanitarians. A weakness is inconstancy accompanied by a total disregard for the feelings of others.

7 DIVINATION AND DARK DEITIES

O Lady Moon, your horns point to the East
Shine, be increased!
O Lady Moon, your horns point to the West;
Wane, be at rest!
— CHRISTINA ROSSETTI

A Moon Primer

Once long ago humans depended upon the moon for reckoning time, planting crops and harvesting the sea. Its phases and its path through the sky were matters of concern and interest to all. Today very few people indeed are even aware, beyond a casual glance, of the moon's presence. In a sense the lovely silver sphere which sometimes

lights our darkness is more mysterious now despite the exploration of its surface. The moon's curious forces continue to exert their influence over us and our planet. We and the oceans of Earth still unceasingly respond to the moon's magnetic appeal. As a symbol of mystic signifi-

cance, appreciated by so many ancient religious expressions, the moon remains as potent as ever, at least to the poet, the artist, and the witch.

The moon like the sun rises in the east and sets in the west. Unlike the sun, its size and shape continually change. Four cycles of approximately seven days each total a lunar month, which forms the basis for our present calendar system. The ancients held that the day began at nightfall, and the custom of celebrating holidays on their eve echoes the old tradition.

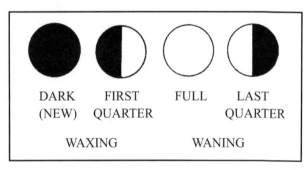

DARK (NEW)   FIRST QUARTER   FULL   LAST QUARTER

WAXING   WANING

The slender crescent appearing soon after dark-of-the-moon is called, obviously enough, the new moon. It waxes, grows larger, to the first quarter visible in the sky as a half-moon. The quarter in this instance refers to the sequence of the four phases. As the moon waxes, its horns point to the east until it reaches full circle. The waning moon diminishes in size, horns pointing west, until we see no moon at all.

The times of rising and setting relate to the phases according to a definite pattern, as recorded in this old country rhyme:

> *A new moon rises with the sun,*
> *Its waxing half at midday shows,*
> *The full moon climbs at sunset hour,*
> *And waning half the midnight knows.*

68

Woodcut from *Wirkungen der Planten* (1470) depicts the world under lunar domination

Luna, Roman Moon Goddess   Hans Sebald Beham (1530)

Moon Lore

Goddesses of the Moon

The moon is primarily associated with female deities. Isis and Hathor were identified with the crescent moon in Egyptian spiritual belief. The Phoenicians called their goddess Astarte, the Queen of Heaven with crescent horns. The Greek goddess Artemis, lover of woods and the wild chase, was symbolized by the moon — known in varying aspects as Phoebe, Selene and Cynthia. Romans named their moon goddess Diana, Luna, and Lucina when she governed the sea tides. And before all deities of the moon pantheon is the primitive concept of the mysterious Hecate. She represents the moon before rising, after setting, and for the three nights when the moon is lost from sight — the awesome goddess of witchcraft. Robert Graves's study *The White Goddess* illuminates other lunar cults and adds the names Leucothea from pre-Aryan Europe and Ngame, the African Triple Moon-goddess.

The Moon and the Sun

That our planet has a single moon to light the night and oppose the sun by day has undoubtedly led to human themes of duality. Forces called good and evil, certainty and chance, instinct and reason have been dramatized in art and religion from the beginning of recorded time. Through these expressions we can see that everything involves its opposite and that ultimately they form one whole. An understanding of the twofold truth is an essential in achieving harmony, the mystic awareness of one's place in the cosmos.

The Witch   Hans Weiditz (1532)

Moons of Leo and Virgo   Paris (1499)

The Moon's Place

The position of the moon in the zodiac at the time of your birth has
a direct bearing on your instinctive behavior, habits, response to
the environment in which you live, and inherited characteristics.

An Aries moon at your birth lends courage and a reckless
nature.

If your moon sign is Taurus, stability and determination
are present.

To be born under the Gemini moon foretells liveliness
and versatility.

Sensitivity, tenacity and originality are gifts of a Cancer
moon.

Leo's moon brings with it strength, self-confidence and
creativity.

The moon sign of Virgo bestows discrimination and
meticulousness.

The influence of the moon in Libra adds idealism and a
bit of indolence.

When your moon sign is Scorpio, you are proud, moody
and possessive.

A Sagittarian moon connotes intuitive power and a
certain restlessness.

Capricorn's moon in your horoscope grants patience and
a cautious nature.

An Aquarian moon sign indicates compassion and a touch
of eccentricity.

Imagination and a loving spirit grace those born under
the moon in Pisces.

71

William Blake's painting of Hecate

HECATE

Goddess of Night is a title often given to Hecate, whose threefold aspect as patroness of witchcraft dates back at least three thousand years. Later, in Greek literature of the classical period, she sometimes merged or was associated with other goddess concepts: Selene, the moon in the sky; Artemis, the huntress on earth; and Persephone, queen of the underworld. Hecate was acknowledged as most powerful, claiming occult matters as her particular domain.

Hecate's worship may have arisen in Thrace, a wild and mysterious region of northern Greece renowned for its sorcery. Another theory contends that the conception of the dark goddess originated in Asia Minor. She belongs to an earlier order of divinities than the Olympians. Hecate's themes were old at the time of Homer--her savagery, her triple form symbolizing control over heaven, earth and sea, and her devotion to beasts are characteristics of archaic deities. All black creatures were sacred to Hecate. Coal-black dogs were her constant companions and nearly every ancient reference mentions these animals:

Hark! Hark! her hounds are baying through the town.
Where three roads meet, there she is standing.

The Greeks considered crossroads to be places of uncanny power and ghostly activity. Statues of Hecate in triple form were often placed there in order that the goddess could watch all three paths simultaneously. The threefold theme is apparent in her Latin name, Trivia. Her appearance as frightening apparition to travelers who dared to walk the night roads is a common motif in Greek and Roman tales. Hecate's symbols include a key and a lighted torch. Both signify the possession of hidden knowledge and indicate a gleam of light in Hecate's darkness. The Homeric Hymn to Demeter mentions Hecate as the only immortal to hear Persephone's cry for help when she was abducted by Hades.

Hecate's aid is often enlisted by witches and necromancers. Ovid has Medea invoke her:

Have I not reason, beldams as you are,
Saucy and overbold? How did you dare
To trade and traffic with Macbeth
In riddles and affairs of death;
And I, the mistress of your charms,
The close contriver of all harms,
Was never call'd to bear my part,
Or show the glory of our art?

O night, faithful preserver of mysteries, and ye bright stars, whose golden beams with the moon succeed the fires of day; thou three-formed Hecate, who knowest our undertakings and comest to our aid; ye spells and arts that wise men use.

In the Orphic literature of the third century A. D., Hecate answers the call of a supplicant by emerging from her cave, wearing on her head a wreath of oak leaves entwined with deadly serpents. The hounds of the goddess howl and their glistening black forms are seen in the flickering torchlight.

Memories of Hecate survived for centuries. In a familiar scene from Macbeth, Shakespeare recounts the stormy meeting on the heath where the three prophetic witches meet Hecate and she berates them:

The Hecate Wheel

Emblem of the eternity of witchcraft and a mystic symbol used to invoke the dark goddess from ancient times. Its threefold pattern in a never-ending circle is used for contemplation and trance-inducement in Western mysticism.

Aubrey Beardsley

"Tell me about Pan… with his goat's feet and two horns… Through wooded glades he wanders with dancing nymphs who foot it on some sheer cliff's edge, calling upon Pan, the shepherd-god, long-haired, unkempt… Often he courses through the glistening high mountains, and often, on the shouldered hills he speeds along slaying wild beasts, this keen-eyed god."

Homeric Hymn to Pan

Persephone

"Persephone, daughter of Demeter, the goddess of fertility, was gathering flowers with her companions in a sheltered valley where spring is everlasting. There she was seen by the king of the underworld, Hades, who was examining the foundations of Sicily, fearful that earthquakes might have opened the earth's crust and let light into his dark realm. He loved the maiden at sight and bore her away in his chariot drawn by black steeds to his kingdom of the dead beneath the earth."

Ovid, *Metamorphoses, V*

"When Demeter learned that Persephone had vanished, she sought her daughter throughout the earth. But there was no trace of the girl, and in her sorrow Demeter neglected to watch over the crops, casting a blight over the whole land. At last Arethusa spoke from her river and told of seeing Persephone being carried off to the underworld.

"Demeter begged Zeus to have Persephone restored to her. The king of the gods agreed that her daughter should go down for the third part of the circling year to darkness and gloom, but for the two parts should live with her mother and the other deathless gods. And so each spring, when Persephone arises, pleasant weather comes and living things begin to grow on earth after the dark winter."

Homeric Hymn to Demeter

Artemis (Diana) prepares the altar for divination. From a copper plaque in the Delos Museum, 3rd century B.C.

THE MEANS OF DIVINATION

Aeromancy, by the air
Alectryomancy, by cocks eating grain
Anthroposcopy, by facial features
Arithmancy, by numbers
Astrology, by the heavenly bodies
Belomancy, by arrows
Bibliomancy, by random choice in a book
Botanomancy, by herbs
Capnomancy, by smoke
Carromancy, by melting wax
Cartomancy, by cards
Catoptromancy, by mirrors
Cattabomancy, by vessels of brass
Cheiromancy, by the hands
Cleromancy, by dice
Crystallomancy, by a crystal
Dactylomancy, by finger-rings
Demonomancy, by demons
Geomancy, by earth
Gyromancy, by whirling in a circle

Hydromancy, by water
Icthyomancy, by fishes
Idolomancy, by an image
Lampadomancy, by candle flame
Lithomancy, by stones
Livanomancy, by inhaling incense
Macharomancy, by knives or swords
Necromancy, by consulting ghosts
Oniromancy, by dreams
Onomatomancy, by names
Ornithomancy, by bird's flight
Pessomancy, by pebbles
Psychomancy, by the soul
Psychometry, by touching an object
Pyromancy, by gazing into fire
Rhabdomancy, by divining rod
Sciomancy, by shadows
Spodomancy, by ashes
Theomancy, by oracle
Zoomancy, by animal behavior

Mirror, Mirror

The art of divining the future through auto-hypnosis in a mirror appears throughout the history of Western mysticism. A votary of the goddess Demeter gazed into a sacred spring to predict the harvest. Pythagoras, in the manner of the Thessalian sorcerers, held a disc of polished metal up to the moon before reading its message. It has been said that Catherine de Medici, a reputed witch, relied on mirror divination to guide her through the tangled affairs of state in sixteenth-century France.

The Grimorium Verum, published in 1517, includes directions on divining by the Mirror of Solomon. The ceremony takes more than forty-five days and requires strict disipline and a ritual of prayer over a "shining and well-polished plate of fine steel." Before one scorns the exactitude of the old books of ceremonial magic, it is wise to consider the possibility of their allegorical character. We know precise rites enable the adept to "still" the mind

to the proper degree for the performance of an act of magic. Even a natural witch depends on ceremony and ritual in order to achieve the desired results.

A full-length three-paneled mirror is a versatile aid to the modern witch. In mastering astral projection, it often proves to be a more effective tool than a single mirror. The curved surface of the human eye permits us to see to the side as well as to the front, and with three reflected images our vision can comprehend the whole body more clearly. Before retiring for the night, look directly into your own eyes in the center panel. When you reach a state of semi-trance, go to bed. You will find that the threefold you merges into one actuality and seems to gaze down on you from above. With this realization, projection is but another short step.

The three-paneled mirror serves the art of catoptromancy as well. For a glimpse into the future, privacy in the quiet of night is advised. Darken the room, and before each of the mirror's three panels place a lighted candle. Position yourself so you can stare fixedly at the reflected image of the center candle flame. When a state of self-hypnosis is attained blow out the middle candle. Your breath will cloud the glass. Surrender to the experience, for it is a mistake to try too hard. Relax and allow a series of visions to come as they will. Through half-closed eyes you may see future events unfold there in the mirror.

A third use of the three-paneled mirror is as enlightening to the mortal as it is to the witch. Seeing three images allows you to catch an unexpected view which is more accurate than prolonged study in a single looking-glass. There is no better way to discover your own essence. Fashion has an unfortunate way of maneuvering an individual into unsuitable styles. Cast a cold eye on the three reflections of you. Depend on instinct and sense of self to provide good judgement. Discard from your wardrobe all the garments, no matter how serviceable, that are not becoming. Try a variety of hair styles until you find the right one. Determine to rise above current fads and be yourself. When your image suits your essence, you are in harmony — happier and better able to use the gifts granted to you.

The Occult Palm

Cheiromancy, palmistry, is one of the most difficult to master of all the divinatory arts. The rules are many and require extensive study as well as an excellent memory. The experience gained from examining many hands soon teaches that for every rule there is an exception. Finally reward comes as an intuitive sense takes over to guide your effort, and soon each palm reveals its message clearly.

Both palms tell a story. If you are righthanded, your left is called the dreamer, and on it is written your destiny. The right or working hand, discloses how chance and your will have altered fate. And so the working palm changes as the years pass.

The major lines of Life, Head, and Heart are found on every palm. The shape of the hands, their movement, minor lines, mounts and markings as well as their clarity, conjunctions and placements are all factors to be considered in a reading.

There are certain signs that are said to reveal occult traits. It is seldom that all appear on a single palm, but the presence of any one of these indicates the potential ability in the practice of the secret arts.

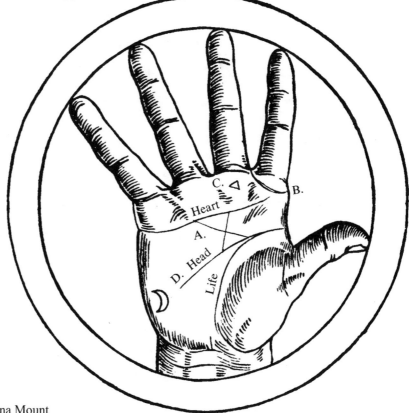

A. The Mystic Cross
B. Ring of Solomon
C. Triangle on the Mount of Saturn
D. Head Line pointing toward the Luna Mount

8 ASTROLOGICAL LORE

We are born at a given moment, in a given place, and like vintage wines
we have the qualities of the year and of the season in which we are born.
— C. G. JUNG

The characteristics assigned to each sign of the zodiac derived from centuries-old lore and legend. The Chaldeans first identified the constellations in their present order as early as 2500 B.C. But the Greeks in the centuries preceding the Christian era named the circle of animals the zodiac. They wove myths around the signs and bestowed many of the correspondences astrologers use today. Evidence indicates that many ancient systems of astrology, including Egyptian, Indian and even Chinese, were influenced by Greek thought.

Ancient astrology's enduring gift is the exquisite beauty of its celestial patterns.

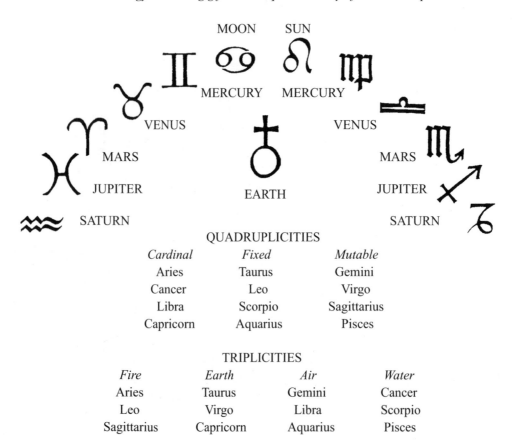

QUADRUPLICITIES

Cardinal	Fixed	Mutable
Aries	Taurus	Gemini
Cancer	Leo	Virgo
Libra	Scorpio	Sagittarius
Capricorn	Aquarius	Pisces

TRIPLICITIES

Fire	Earth	Air	Water
Aries	Taurus	Gemini	Cancer
Leo	Virgo	Libra	Scorpio
Sagittarius	Capricorn	Aquarius	Pisces

Gems of the Zodiac

The custom of adorning oneself with gems to complement the seasons had assumed popularity in Europe by the eighteenth century. Jewelers cast about for a source of information to establish what birthstones applied for each month. Not surprisingly they looked to the Bible for authority. A reference from the Old Testament and one from the New Testament served their purpose. The first was the description of the jewels in the breastplate of Aaron, high priest of the Jews, in Exodus 28: 17-20. This proved unreliable, for the order and translations of gem names were disputed then as now by biblical scholars. The second, based on the listing of jewels adorning the wall of the New Jerusalem, Apocalypse 21: 19-20, seemed to be firmer ground. This sequence had already been successfully applied to other groups of twelve. In those days the year began in March, so the order was determined as jasper, sapphire, chalcedony, emerald, sardonyx, sardius, chrysolite, beryl, topaz, chrysoprase, jacinth and amethyst.

The birthstones regarded today as traditional were actually assigned in 1912 at a meeting of the National Association of Retail Jewelers in Kansas City. These correspondences seem based on commercialism and, in some instances, mere whimsy; investigation proves there was little validity for their choices. The Kansas City convention drew on the two biblical sources, borrowed from Arabic and Hindu traditions, and was influenced by a popular tome, *The Light of Egypt*. As these lists had been previously assigned to zodiac signs, the shift to months cause odd transitions. It is clear that the contemporary birthstone scheme evolved more from accidental sequence than logical correspondences.

Agrippa's choice of zodiacal stones in his *On Occult Philosophy* is marked by the careful thought of a scholar and metaphysician. The birthstones according to Agrippa:

Aries — SARDONYX
Taurus — CARNELIAN
Gemini — TOPAZ
Cancer — CHALCEDONY
Leo — JASPER
Virgo — EMERALD
Libra — BERYL
Scorpio — AMETHYST
Sagittarius — SAPPHIRE
Capricorn — CHYRSOPRASE
Aquarius — CRYSTAL
Pisces — LAPIS LAZULI

ARIES

March 21 — April 20

ARIES — the Ram

A Greek king of long ago grew tired of his wife. He left her to marry another, and his two children felt threatened by the evil designs of their stepmother. This wicked queen prevented the harvest by parching the seed-corn. Then she bribed a messenger to say the Oracle declared crops would not grow until the king's son and daughter were sacrificed. When the terrified children lay upon the sacrificial altar, the god Hermes sent a wondrous ram with fleece of gold to rescue them. As the ram bore the children to safety, Helle, the princess, fell and was drowned in the sea which bears her name—the Hellespont. Phrixus, the prince, found refuge in Colchis, where he was kindly received. In gratitude for his deliverance, Phrixus sacrificed the ram to Zeus and presented its fleece to the king of Colchis. The Golden Fleece would later become the prize of Jason and the Argonaut expedition.

Aries is a fire sign marked by courage and self-sacrifice. Under the rulership of Mars, Arians enjoy nothing more than an idealistic quest.

BORN UNDER ARIES

poet, Baudelaire
painter, Goya
author, Henry James
star, Charlie Chaplin
composer, Bach
philosopher, Descartes
head of state, Thomas Jefferson

Aries — SARDONYX

Most of the lovely cameo ornaments long treasured by women are created from sardonyx. The name of the gem derives from its two sources — deep reddish-orange sard from Sardis, capital of ancient Lydia, and from the parallel bands of creamy white onyx that run through it to form sardonyx. The gem has a long and bewildering occult history. From earliest recorded time it was prized as a charm to ensure marital bliss. By the classical age sardonyx acquired a reputation for increasing eloquence and was favored by orators. During the Middle Ages, the stone was worn by expectant mothers to prevent premature birth and ward off evil influences. A sardonyx lightly rubbed on the eyelids was believed to stop eyes from watering, a folk remedy still in use.

The red of Mars combined with white for the purity of springtime — a new beginning — suits the sign of Aries well.

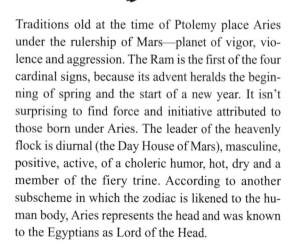

Traditions old at the time of Ptolemy place Aries under the rulership of Mars—planet of vigor, violence and aggression. The Ram is the first of the four cardinal signs, because its advent heralds the beginning of spring and the start of a new year. It isn't surprising to find force and initiative attributed to those born under Aries. The leader of the heavenly flock is diurnal (the Day House of Mars), masculine, positive, active, of a choleric humor, hot, dry and a member of the fiery trine. According to another subscheme in which the zodiac is likened to the human body, Aries represents the head and was known to the Egyptians as Lord of the Head.

TAURUS

April 21 — May 21

TAURUS — the Bull

Aphrodite, goddess of love, mischievously had her son Eros shoot an arrow of desire into the heart of Zeus as he casually watched the beautiful maiden Europa gathering wildflowers near the sea. The smitten Zeus, ever wary of Hera, his jealous wife, cautiously disguised himself as a marvelous bull before approaching Europa. Charmed by the gentleness and beauty of the divine bull, Europa trustingly mounted his broad back. After he had borne her over the sea to his beloved isle of Crete, Zeus reassumed his godlike form. Europa and Zeus lived there in happy adultery, raising fine sons, and Hera was none the wiser.

The myth is a love story with a happy ending and the sign of Taurus echoes its felicity. A sign of Earth governed by the planet Venus and the goddess of love, Taureans are romantic, cautious, home-loving and blessed with serenity. The nobility of spirit often attributed to this sign reflects the quality of Zeus, greatest of all the gods.

BORN UNDER TAURUS

poet, Tagore
painter, Braque
author, Vladimir Nabokov
star, Audrey Hepburn
composer, Brahms
philosopher, Kierkegaard
head of state, Cromwell

Taurus — CARNELIAN

Ancient Persians wore amulets set with this deep reddish-brown stone, for they believed it possessed power in itself. The curious cylinder-seals of the Assyrians when cut in carnelian assured the bearer protection from evil spirits. Egyptians treasured the gem and their sacred heart amulet, the *ab*, was traditionally carved from it. The name derives from the Latin *carneus*, meaning "of the flesh." Possibly because of its color, medieval folk medicine called the carnelian a "blood stone," prescribing it to stop nosebleeds and clear the skin of minor eruptions. People with uncontrollable tempers were advised to wear the stone, for its touch repressed rage. Curiously, the surface of the carnelian does not hold heat, making the stone popular as engraved signet rings, for the cool carnelian stamps a sharp impression in hot sealing wax.

Themes of serenity, peace and love surround both the sign of Taurus and the gem Agrippa chose as its correspondent.

Nocturnal, feminine, negative, passive, calm, cold, dry, and earthy are qualities assigned to Taurus by the ancient astrologers. The second sign of the zodiac reigns during the height of the spring season and for this reason is designated as fixed, indicating stability. Key words such as patient, placid, and reliable have been used for over two thousand years to describe Taureans. Sensuality, creativity, and a deep appreciation of beauty are gifts of the love goddess, for Taurus occupies the Night House of Venus. In the macrocosm-microcosm system of Ptolemy, Taurus corresponds to the human neck.

GEMINI

May 22 — June 21

GEMINI — the Twins

Within this constellation are two brilliant stars Castor and Pollux, "the heavenly twins." The Greeks knew them as the Dioscuri, meaning "the striplings of Zeus." Their genealogy is as resplendid as their light. The twins' mother Leda, Queen of Sparta, was wooed by Zeus, whom she spurned. Ever resourceful, the God of Gods visited her in the form of a soft, gleaming swan who proved irresistible. In Greek mythology, such things happen. Castor and Pollux issued from this strange union, although some tales call them half-brothers, with the King of Sparta the father of Castor. But all the legends note their brotherly devotion. When Castor was slain, Pollux was inconsolable and the Olympian gods allowed him to join his brother in death.

Gemini, ruled by the planet Mercury and corresponding to the element of air, is often charged with instability. The steadfast loyalty of the heavenly twins tempers this trait. The twins have associations with the messenger god Hermes/Mercury. And because Castor and Pollux were kind to the witch Medea, themes of mystery and magic often accompany interpretations of Gemini.

BORN UNDER GEMINI

poet, Walt Whitman
painter, Gauguin
author, Thomas Hardy
star, Marilyn Monroe
composer, Wagner
philosopher, Jean Paul Sartre
head of state, John F. Kennedy

The Day House of Mercury belongs to the Twins. Nimble mind, quick tongue, and sharp wit are gifts bestowed by Mercury, swiftest of planets and god of communication and curiousity. As Gemini is overhead when spring gives way to summer, it is called mutable, signifying a time of change. Diurnal, masculine, positive, active, cheerful, hot, moist, and the first of the three Air signs describe Gemini by classical interpretation. These qualities give rise to the restless, changeable, unpredictable nature assigned to Gemini by modern astrologers. As the first human and dual image of the zodiac, the Twins receive credit for family devotion along with charges of duplicity. Gemini represents the arms of the zodiacal man.

Gemini — TOPAZ

The topaz of ancient time may have been the peridot or olivine, a brilliant yellow-green gem prized for its hardness. The name "topaz" comes from an island in the Red Sea called *Topazos* (to seek) by Greek mariners, for it was often shrouded in fog and difficult to find. The hidden isle was rich in deposits of peridot. By the Middle Ages the clear yellow gem we know today as topaz had assumed not only the name but all the mystic connotations heretofore assigned to the peridot. Babylonians and Egyptians believed the gem enabled its wearer to tame wild beasts and fend off evil spirits. Medieval lore advised that the topaz be set in gold with an accompanying pearl and worn only on the left side of the body. During the Renaissance the topaz was worn as an amulet of protection against anger and revenge.

The topaz is actually two gems with one history and relates well with the Twins.

CANCER

June 22 — July 23

CANCER — the Crab

Hera, always described as "the jealous wife of Zeus," had plenty to be jealous about. She particularly detested Hercules, a son of Zeus by one of her husband's numerous lovers. When Hercules was engaged in his horrendous battle with the nine-headed Hydra, Hera sent a sea crab to bite Hecules on the heel. For such obedience, Hera rewarded the crab by placing it in the heavens as a constellation.

The crab has odd characteristics—a sidelong gait, a home on its back, casting the shell as it grows. Such curious features as well as the fierce loyalty displayed in the Hydra myth often appear as characteristics astrologically assigned to Cancer. Cancerians belong to the moon and correspond to the element of water; they are regarded as nomadic, secretive and evasive. People born under this sign are faithful to friends and can always be counted on to perform bravely in time of crisis.

BORN UNDER CANCER

poet, Stephen Vincent Benét
painter, Rembrandt
author, Proust
star, Lena Horne
composer, Carl Orff
philosopher, Thoreau
head of state, Julius Caesar

Cancer — CHALCEDONY

Chalcedony (pronounced kal-SED-uh-nee) is a translucent quartz varying in color from milky white to pale blue-gray or warm fawn. An age-old occult use for the gem was to cheer melancholy spirits. Talismans carved from chalcedony were believed to counteract dispiriting influences of the planet Saturn. Romans wore the stone as protection from the Evil Eye. Its waxlike luster calls to mind an image of the moon, and many Gnostic amulets of chalcedony were engraved with the moon's symbol. Seamen from all quarters of the Mediterranean cherished the gem as a protection against drowning. European folk medicine claimed the touch of calcedony upon the brow reduced fever, granted tranquillity and speeded recovery from illness.

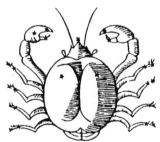

Cancer alone owns the Mansion of the Moon. All anciently assigned qualities reflect the influence of the ruler of the night. Nocturnal, feminine, negative, passive, cold, moist, melancholy, Cancer is the cardinal Water sign and marks the beginning of summer. Its qualities intepret as the intuitive, emotional, mysterious, compelling personality defined for the Crab. Restlessness and a need to be on the move come from lunar aspects. Perhaps the moon — symbol of magic, madness and love — guides the destiny of those born under her sway. Cancer in the zodiacal human form is likened to the breast.

Associations with the moon and the sea belong to the sign of Cancer as they do to its gemstone, the chalcedony.

LEO

July 24 — August 23

LEO — the Lion

The first of the twelve labors of Hercules was to slay the lion of Nemea, a formidable beast no weapons could wound. Hercules with his great strength and abundant self-confidence managed to choke the lion to death. To honor the courage of the Nemean lion in defeat, Zeus placed him in the heavens as a constellation.

Leo, considered by many contemporary astrologers to be the most important sign of the zodiac, is assigned the dignity and brave heart of the king of beasts. Placed under the rulership of the sun and associated with the element of fire, Leonian characteristics are pride, fierceness and impetuosity. But as the myth foretells, the lion can be overwhelmed by a surfeit of his own qualities.

BORN UNDER LEO

poet, Shelley
painter, Thomas Eakins
author, Aldous Huxley
star, Madonna
composer, Debussy
philosopher, Morris Cohen
head of state, Napoleon

Leo — JASPER

Jasper is an opaque, very hard variety of quartz that takes a high polish. The gem occurs in many colors and is usually streaked with other hues: dark green, grass green, terracotta red, brown, warm gray, blue or black. Green jasper was thought to impart wisdom and courage and was especially prized as an amulet by the ancient Persians. A reputation as a bringer of rain and protection from snakebite belonged to green jasper by classical times. The Egyptians called red jasper the blood of Isis, and during the Ptolemaic period it was prized as an amulet worn to secure the favor of the goddess. Powdered jasper of any color was used as an ingredient in Roman love potions guaranteed to ensure constancy. A multicolored jasper bead was suspended on a chain and worn around the neck as a charm of protection dating back to the Middle Ages.

Throughout antiquity the astrological sign of Leo was ever identified with the sun. Sole occupant of the House of the Sun, it is said that the Lion will always advance in life because his ruler never retrogrades. As the fixed sign of the fiery trine, Leo presides over the height of summer matching the maximum heat and light of the sun. Choleric (fiery) humor, masculine gender, positive and active nature, hot, dry and naturally diurnal describe the sign's attributes. Powerful, vital, dominating personality with a weakness for flattery defines Leo. In correspondence to the microcosm the Lion relates to the center of the human solar system, the heart.

The strength and vital color of jasper corresponds nobly with Leo, sign of the lion and the sun.

Virgo

August 24 — September 23

VIRGO — the Virgin

According to classical sources, Greeks and Romans held this birth sign as most favorable. It is likely that the Virgin represents Persephone, daughter of the earth goddess Demeter. The myth of the maiden abducted by Hades, Demeter's grief and the subsequent resolution that Persephone must spend one third of the year in the dark underground kingdom of her captor is a seasonal allegory. Another theory identifies the Virgin as Astraea, the star maiden, who left earth in dismay at the beginning of the Iron Age. Astraea is portrayed holding scales of judgement, but Persephone carries a sheaf of grain, an emblem of harvest, linking her with the sign of Virgo.

The charactaristic dependability assigned to Virgo bears out the harvest theme. An Earth sign governed by the planet Mercury, Virgo has a strain of melancholy as if anticipating the seasonal sojourn to the dark realm below.

BORN UNDER VIRGO

poet, Coleridge
painter, Arp
author, D.H. Lawrence
star, Greta Garbo
composer, Shostakovich
philosopher, John Locke
head of state, Elizabeth I

The Virgin who holds in her left hand a sheaf of grain and in her right, the caduceus wand of Hermes/Mercury has been venerated by many cultures. It is fitting that Virgo reigns as summer ends. Although a mutable sign, one that spans two seasons, the Virgin is astrologically defined as adaptable rather than unstable, because she belongs to the steadfast trine of Earth. Nocturnal, feminine, negative, passive, cold, dry, and calm of nature describe the maiden who became queen of the underworld kingdom. Virgo owns the Night Mansion of Mercury and his quicksilver gifts lend mental agility and deftness. Virgo, the practical one, corresponds to the stomach of the zodiacal man.

Virgo — EMERALD

"Take the stone which is called Smaragdus, in English speech, the emerald. It makes a man to understand well, and gives to him a good memory, augments the riches of him who bears it, and if any man shall hold it under his tongue, he shall prophesy anon." This advice comes from *The Boke of Secrets* by the famed medieval occultist Albertus Magnus. The brilliant green variety of clear beryl is one of the costliest gems and has long been prized by sorcerers. Beyond those attributes listed by the renowned Albertus we find the gem used to drive away evil, to assist in childbirth and preserve chastity as well as to benefit eyesight. The last might well have proceeded from the fact that the Egyptian amulet, the Eye of Horus, symbolic of resurrection, was most often carved in emerald.

Its choice for the sign of Virgo was inspired, for its color carries out the renewal theme of Persephone's annual return in springtime.

LIBRA

September 24 — October 23

LIBRA — the Balance

Libra is deemed by many modern astrologers to be the most desirable of all the zodiac signs. Long ago once part of Scorpio and called *Chelae*, the claws, Libra today is the only inanimate sign in the circle of animals. An age-old occult tale supposes that once Virgo and Scorpio were one sign and Libra was placed between them to separate the male from the female. The representation of scales may support the theory of Virgo as Astraea, who personified divine justice.

Of the Air element and ruled by Venus, Libran traits reflect these correspondences as well as the symbolic scales. It is noteworthy that the scales are often graphically portrayed as out of balance. Seekers of harmony and equity yet destined to be denied both seems to be the fate accorded those born under the mysterious sign of Libra.

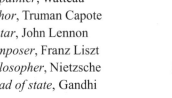

BORN UNDER LIBRA

poet, T.S. Eliot
painter, Watteau
author, Truman Capote
star, John Lennon
composer, Franz Liszt
philosopher, Nietzsche
head of state, Gandhi

The days and nights on Earth are of equal length at the autumnal equinox. A cardinal sign occurring at this time of year is appropriately called the Balance. Some early zodiac art depicts a man holding the scales in perfect balance, but since the Middle Ages Libra's image has been scales alone — often wildly out of balance. Ancient astrologers defined Libra as masculine, positive, active, light-hearted, hot, moist, and one of the airy triplicity. These qualities do not suggest composure nor does Libra's placement in the Day House of Venus. In classical times the influence of Venus over an Air sign was considered a mixed blessing, for instinctive pleasure can often become self-indulgence. Libra relates to the hips of Ptolemy's zodiacal figure.

Libra — BERYL

The beryl gem is a transparent mineral of excellent hardness, most often of a blue-green color, commonly called the aquamarine by modern lapidaries. Although beryl occurs in other colors, it is the "sea green" variety that the ancient world held in high esteem as a charm to banish fear. At sea it gave protection from a raging storm, and in battle its touch made a warrior invincible. Medieval texts held that beryl quickened the intellect and provided a sure cure for laziness. A couple, long married, might reawaken lost desire by acquiring a fine beryl. And as a scrying stone the gem was considered peerless by no less an authority than the great Renaissance magician Paracelsus.

As much of Libra falls in October, the eighth month of the Roman calender, and beryl and the number eight have a long mystic association, the choice of this gem as correspondent is clear.

SCORPIO

October 24 — November 22

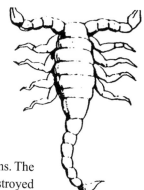

SCORPIO — the Scorpion
The mighty hunter Orion foolishly boasted that he would kill every animal on earth. Diana, goddess of the moon and the hunt, overheard his threat and sent a scorpion to sting him to death. Zeus honored the creature by setting it in the sky and at Diana's request placed Orion close by.

Scorpio, ruled by Mars and Pluto and associated with the element of Water, is one of the strongest and most maligned of signs. The scorpion is nocturnal, for it can be destroyed by the tropical sun. As a creature of night favored by Diana, mysterious magic powers influence Scorpio's attributes. Its myth reveals the characteristics of a ruthless, revengeful nature so often ascribed to this zodiac sign. Protector of its animal kin, the Scorpion is a dangerous enemy but a dependable ally in any quest requiring courage.

BORN UNDER SCORPIO

poet, Dylan Thomas
painter, Monet
author, Dostoyevsky
star, Vivien Leigh
composer, Paul Hindemith
philosopher, Albert Camus
head of state, Nehru

Scorpio — AMETHYST
The name of the clear purple or blue-violet variety of crystallized quartz comes from the Greek word *amethystos*, meaning "not to be intoxicated." It was the jewel worn by the high priest during initiation rites of the Eleusinian Mysteries, for it prevented him from becoming "confused, distracted or overwhelmed by the intense fascination of external phenomena." The usual interpretation that the amethyst was merely a means to avoid drunkeness falls far short of its original significance. The secrets of Eleusis were never revealed, but over time Dionysus, god of wine, was worshipped there. During the Middle Ages the amethyst became associated with sacrifice as well as wine. In this context the gem was an amulet of protection for both hunter and soldier. An amethyst placed under the pillow was believed to bring a sleeper prophetic dreams and ensure the memory of them.

The ancients placed Scorpio in the Night Mansion of Mars. When Pluto was discovered in 1930, modern astrologers asserted that the zodiac sign of death and regeneration belonged to Hades/Pluto, dread Lord of the Underworld. The mystery still surrounding the planet Pluto allows Scorpio to continue possessing Martian traits of courage, discipline and self-control. Nocturnal and feminine, Scorpio is the fixed sign of the watery trine. Cold, moist, negative, passive, melancholy qualities form the intense, secretive, passionate and relentless character ascribed to the Scorpion. An alternative symbol for midautumn's sign is the eagle. Scorpio relates to the sexual organs or, as they were commonly called in Victorian texts, the "secret parts."

In Agrippa's time, Scorpio marked the grape harvest and the slaughter of animals for winter provision, combining wine and sacrifice, twin characteristics of the god Dionysus and the amethyst jewel.

Sagittarius

November 23 — December 21

SAGITTARIUS — the Archer

Personified as a centaur, half man and half horse, the Archer may recall the Greeks' first glimpse of mounted troops. Horsemanship was unknown in Greece at the time of Homer. Of all the fabulous creatures of antiquity, the centaur alone is accorded good traits. The constellation of Sagittarius represents Chiron, the wisest of all centaurs. Instructed by Apollo and Artemis, Chiron was revered for his ability in hunting, music and medicine as well as for his gift of prophecy. An acknowledged sage and excellent teacher, the centaur Chiron was placed among the stars upon his death.

Sagittarius is ruled by Zeus/Jupiter, the most powerful of all the gods. Fire is the element of the Archer, and forthrightness is a major personality trait. Wisdom, goodness and sound judgement reflect the qualities of the Chiron myth. And skill in foretelling the future is often attributed to those born under the sign of Sagittarius.

BORN UNDER SAGITTARIUS

poet, Emily Dickinson
painter, Seurat
author, Mark Twain
star, Jimi Hendrix
composer, Beethoven
philosopher, Spinoza
head of state, Winston Churchill

Babylonian inscriptions from the dawn of history refer to this sign as the Strong One. Power, magnanimity and mercy are traits of those who dwell in the Day House of Jupiter, ruler of the gods. As the only figure of the zodiac that combines man and beast, the Archer bestows great affinity for all living creatures. Classical astrology classifies Sagittarius as masculine, diurnal, positive, active, hot, dry and of cheerful nature. The archer is a member of the fiery trine but mutability lends an elusive inconstancy to an otherwise noble character. Understandable because the Archer rules when autumn gives way to winter. Sagittarius is related to the thighs of the zodiacal man.

Sagittarius — SAPPHIRE

The word sapphire derives from the Sanskrit meaning "deep blue" and in ancient texts probably refers to lapis lazuli — for *sapphiros* were described as opaque with golden flecks. The precious stone of clear blue corundum was little known in Europe before the twelfth century. It quickly gained renown as one of the most powerful and sacred jewels in the art of magic. Occultists claimed the sapphire allowed them to understand the most obscure oracles. "Wytches love well this stone for they werke certen wonders by its vertue," wrote a fifteenth-century author. Sapphire acquired a reputation as an antidote against poison and a disperser of evil spirits. Albertus Magnus advised that a sapphire if dipped in cold water and placed on the eye would surely remove all foreign matter and impurities.

Sagittarius belongs to Jupiter, mightiest of gods, and the sapphire's power was believed to surpass that of all other gems.

CAPRICORN

December 22 — January 20

CAPRICORN — the Goat

Capricornus is derived from the Latin *caper*, a goat, and *cornu*, a horn. The sign is graphically portrayed as a sea-goat having the forepart of a goat and the hindpart of a dolphin. The goat belongs to Dionysus, the god of carefree abandon, while the dolphin is the creature of Apollo, god of moderation and truth. As no myth illuminates the sign of Capricorn, the symbolism of the sea-goat reveals a fact of life cherished by the Greeks; that is people must balance the duality of their natures in order to achieve happiness. The sign was regarded in ancient times as one of good omen and called the Southern Gate of the Sun.

Modern astrology makes use of the ruling planet of Saturn to adjudge characteristics of those born under Capricorn. An Earth sign, determined to win at all costs, the goat needs wide range but requires a tether lest he roam in forbidden places.

BORN UNDER CAPRICORN
poet, Edgar Allan Poe
painter, Cezanne
author, Henry Miller
star, Elvis Presley
composer, Puccini
philosopher, William James
head of state, Richard Nixon

The sea-goat lives in the Night House of Saturn and it is from that god's baleful influence that many of Capricorn's negative aspects derive. Saturn was the Roman equivalent of the Greek god Cronus, who destroyed his father Uranus and devoured his own children. The most remote planet in Ptolemy's day, Saturn was likened to the exiled Cronus when Zeus came to power. It fell to the distant Saturn to rule the coldest time of the year. Capricorn's qualities are nocturnal, feminine, negative, passive, phlegmatic, cold, dry, and of the trine of Earth. A cardinal sign because it heralds winter, the Goat is endowed with authority and inventiveness. Capricorn represents the knees of the microcosm.

Capricorn — CHRYSOPRASE

Chrysoprase, from the Greek *chrysos*, gold, and *prason*, leek, is the name for a translucent yellow-green variety of chalcedony. Its fame as a gem of magic spread throughout the ancient world, for it was the talisman of Alexander the Great. The conquerer called it his "victory stone" and wore it sewn in his sash. Pausing to bathe in the Euphrates on his return from the Indian campaign, Alexander unwisely left his sash on the bank. A serpent plucked away the gem and dropped it in the river. The legend tells of Alexander's vain search, loss of confidence, subsequent illness and death at the age of thirty-three at the height of his glory. With the serpent's theft in mind, the chrysoprase would become the amulet of thieves. A nineteenth-century source records that a thief under sentence to be hanged might escape execution if he placed a chrysoprase under his tongue.

The tale of Alexander's loss of good fortune dominates the lore concerning Capricorn's gem. Guard your good luck charm, for the range between glory and hopelessness uniquely suits the qualities of both the sea-goat and Saturn.

Aquarius

January 21 — February 19

AQUARIUS — the Water Bearer

Symbolized by a man pouring water from an urn, Aquarius assumes the role of mankind's benefactor. The only mortal to be included in the zodiac circle, no legend dramatizes his attributes. Wisdom, gentleness and moderation are said to typify the Water-Bearer. A negative aspect of forgetfulness mars the otherwise favorable view of the Aquarian character.

As we are in the Aquarian Age, we can expect to find healing and regeneration. The warning implied suggests that we must sharpen our memories of the past to avoid failure. The Aquarian patience may save the day with a gift of time. A sign of Air, the Water-Bearer is ruled by the planet Uranus, Father Heaven to the Greeks. Those born under Aquarius are said to be blessed with intuitive understanding.

BORN UNDER AQUARIUS

poet, Lord Byron
painter, Manet
author, Dickens
star, Clark Gable
composer, Mozart
philosopher, Francis Bacon
head of state, Abraham Lincoln

Aquarius — CRYSTAL

The ancients believed that the clear colorless quartz found in rock formations was actually petrified ice, and our word crystal derives from the Greek *krystallos*, meaning "clear ice." Rock crystal was not extensively used in the East as a gemstone, but tiny spheres of crystal, set in silver bands to be worn on chains around the neck, have been unearthed in the West—Germany, France, the British Isles and Ireland, wherever the Celtic tribes held sway. Ornaments, scrying stones, amulets? Archaeologists differ as to their use but agree that their presence in royal grave sites clearly indicates the high value placed upon them. Scottish folk legends call the crystal balls Druid stones, claiming they impart healing properties to flowing water. Water charged with the power of the crystal was believed to cure illness in man and beast.

In 1781 a new planet was discovered and named Uranus for the Greek sky-god, father and originator of all living things. Aquarius had belonged in the Day House of Saturn until nineteenth-century astrologers decided that the House of Uranus was a more appropriate lodging. The fixed sign of the airy triplicity is masculine, diurnal, positive, active, cheerful, hot and moist. These characteristics agree with the humanitarian image of the Water-Bearer, who not only brings comfort but displays the explosive, inventive and perceptive traits ascribed to the sky-god. In the "as above, so below" scheme of life, Aquarius corresponds to the human ankles.

Mystic themes of the healing power in flowing water belong to the Water-Bearer, and as the Aquarian quest is to recover lost wisdom, the mysterious crystal is a perfect talisman.

90

PISCES

February 20 — March 20

PISCES — the Fishes

The zodiac sign of Pisces is represented by two fishes joined together by a ribbon of stars. In Greek myth the love deities Aphrodite and her son Eros, basking on the banks of the Euphrates river, were threatened by the sudden appearance of the Typhon, "a flaming monster with a hundred heads." To escape, the pair leaped into the water and assumed the shape of fish.

Pisceans, ruled by Neptune and akin to the element of Water, are prone to shun danger, as did the love goddess and her son. The Fishes are thought to possess mystic sensitivity and are gifted in the art of love, attributes befitting the disguised deities of myth. Avoiding responsibility is a negative characteristic common to those born under the sign of Pisces. Easily defeated in contests of willpower, the elusive fishes may become victims and enjoy the role.

BORN UNDER PISCES

poet, W.H. Auden
painter, Renoir
author, Victor Hugo
star, Elizabeth Taylor
composer, Chopin
philosopher, Schopenhauer
head of state, George Washington

Emotional, mystic, yielding, ever-changing are descriptions occurring in the classical astrological assessment of Pisces. The mutable sign of the watery trine marks the end of winter. Nocturnal, feminine, negative, passive, cold, moist and melancholy are qualities defined for the Fishes. For many centuries the Fishes swam in the Night House of Jupiter, and that god's might and majesty added some stability. But when the planet Neptune was discovered in 1795 and astrologers gave Pisces over to the rulership of the sea-god, the weakness, dreaminess and impressionability of the sign's interpretation greatly increased. Pisces, a dual image, relates to the feet of the microcosm.

Pisces — LAPIS LAZULI

Lapis lazuli (LAP-iss LAZ-you-lie) is from the Latin word *lapis*, a stone, and an Arabic word describing the blue color of the night sky. The opaque gem of deep. rich blue, flecked with tiny particles of gold pyrite likened to stars, was revered in the Near East. To nomadic desert peoples, since earliest time the sun has been an enemy while the moon and night bring blessed relief. The stone of the night sky was sacred to moon divinities of many cultures, and the image of the Egyptian goddess of truth, Maat, was traditionally carved of lapis lazuli. The classical period associated the stone with love and it was worn as an amulet to regain lost affection, cure melancholy and increase sexual vigor.

The gentle mystery of night, repose and love represented by the lapis lazuli is in keeping with the qualities astrology defines for the sign of Pisces.

9 FOOD AND FESTIVALS

Roodmas

The feast known as Roodmas, Beltane, or Walpurgisnacht begins at sundown on May Eve. In essence, the holiday bids welcome to spring and the moon. With ancient ceremony witches bless the awakened land, the water's freedom from its prison of ice. Witches rejoice together as the earth once more dons a mantle of green and the goddess rules again. Bonfires on hilltops, maypole dances, the crowning of a queen and the gathering of dew at dawn are all customs still observed by many without realization of their ancient significance.

Each coven greets spring with its own sacred ritual, but the feast to follow may vary from year to year and may be drawn from any cuisine. The essential parts of a sabbat feast are variety of fare and dishes that can be prepared in advance. Once the food awaits, the cook is free to participate in the sacred ceremony without concern.

This year we celebrate May Eve in Germany, where the holiday is known as Walpurgisnacht. The Brocken, the highest mountain in northern Germany, was the ancient's favorite meeting place, and we asked Margarette Ballweg to plan a buffet menu that might have been en-

joyed there. We include her recipe for *Haselnusscreme*, a dessert of ancient origin.

Gedun Stetes Sauerkraut
Steamed Spiced Sauerkraut

Bohnensalat
Green Bean Salad

Kartoffelsalat mit Speck
Potato Salad with Bacon

Rollmops   *Blut Wurst*
Herring Salad   Blood Sausage
Fresh Ham Slices   Assorted Cold Cuts

Suss-Saure Bratwurst
Pork Sausage with Sweet-Sour Sauce

Freshly baked rye bread and sweet butter complete the spread. And for dessert…

Haselnusscreme
Hazelnut Cream Pudding
2 tablespoons unflavored gelatine
1/2 cup cold water
3 cups hazelnuts, shelled, blanched and ground in
   Cuisinart, blender or by mortar and pestle
3 3/4 cups milk
9 egg yolks
1 1/2 cups sugar
3 teaspoons vanilla extract
3 cups heavy cream

In a heatproof measuring cup, sprinkle gelatine over cold water. When the gelatine has softened for 3 minutes, set the cup in a skillet of simmering water and heat over low flame, stirring, until the gelatine is completely dissolved. Remove cup from skillet and let stand.

Combine nuts and milk in a 6-quart saucepan and heat, stirring constantly, until bubbles form around the edge. Remove from heat.

Beat egg yolks and sugar in a large bowl. Pour the hot milk in a thin stream over the mixture, beating vigorously as you pour. When combined, transfer to the saucepan and over a low flame heat the custard while stirring until it is thick enough to coat the spoon. Do not let the custard come to a boil. Remove from heat, stir in the dissolved gelatine and add vanilla. Transfer to a glass serving bowl and cool to room temperature.

Beat cream until it holds soft peaks. Gently fold into the cooled custard. Hold a small charm of pure silver over the bowl for a moment and say, *Queen of Darkness, honor us this night with thy blessing.* Let the charm fall into the bowl. Refrigerate for 3 hours, or until firm.

Needless to say, the recipient of the silver token can anticipate future joy as well as the immediate pleasure of a delectable dessert.

Lammas

Lammas, August Eve, is the time for wishes. We wish the crops taller, the harvest greater, our love stronger and our spirits higher. This is the time to cast love enchantments, for the magic of Lammas will favor such desires.

Let's imagine ourselves in Italy — Benevento, under the legendary walnut tree. And there we will celebrate the summer sabbat.

> *In Benevento a nut-tree stands*
> *And thither by night from many lands,*
> *Over the waters and on the wind,*
> *Come witches flying of every kind,*
> *On goats, and boars, and bears, and cats,*
> *Some upon broomsticks, some like bats,*
> *Howling, hurtling, hurrying, all,*
> *Come to the tree at the master's call.*

— C.G. Leland, from Dom Piccini's *Ottava della Notte.*

On a large table, preferably round, set out loaves of Italian bread and bowls of sweet butter along with platters of raw vegetables — carrot sticks, celery stalks, scallions, radish roses, green pepper strips, and fresh fennel. Accompany the assortment with cruets of the finest virgin olive oil and wine vinegar. Prosciutto and hard salami slices, garnished with sprigs of Italian parsley and hard-cooked egg slices, form another platter. Sardines mashed in prepared mustard and topped with capers make a delicious spread. Provide ripe and stuffed olives in a nest of ice, marinated artichokes, *caponata*, the eggplant relish available in supermarkets, and stuffed anchovies. Should you care to add a delicacy, try:

Gamberetti

2 pounds of shrimp, cooked, shelled and deveined.

    2 hard-cooked egg yolks

    2 teaspoons prepared mustard

    6 tablespoons olive oil

    Juice of 1/2 lemon

    3/4 cup tomato catsup

    4 tablespoons dry sherry

    4 tablespoons heavy cream

    1/2 teaspoon salt

    Freshly ground black pepper to taste

Mash together egg yolks and mustard. Slowly add oil, alternating with lemon juice until all has been added. Stir in the remaining ingredients. Combine with the shrimp and chill.

Marinated Mushrooms

    1/4 cup olive oil

    3 cloves garlic, crushed

    2 pounds mushrooms, sliced

    1 bay leaf

    7 peppercorns

    1 cup dry white wine

    Juice of 1 lemon

    1/2 teaspoon salt

    Freshly ground black pepper to taste

Heat oil in a skillet over moderate heat and sauté garlic until golden. Add mushrooms, bay leaf and peppercorns, mixing well, and cook for 3 minutes. Stir in wine, lemon juice and salt and pepper. Cover and cook over a low heat for 10 minutes, stirring occasionally. Remove to a bowl and chill.

Italian cheeses ranging from the mild Bel Paese to the sharp Gorgonzola combine with fresh fruit to round out the feast. *Buon appetito!*

A Saxon Feast from a brass, English (1091), which appeared in Richard Warner's *Antiquitates Culinariae*, 1791.

Hallowmas

Hallowmas is the most solemn festival of the witches' year. On November Eve we honor dead souls, bid farewell to the moon and welcome the coming of the sun to rule once more. Those of Celtic tradition call the holiday Samhain and with it mark the beginning of winter — dark of the year. It is curious that this one holiday has retained a lasting hold upon the popular imagination. Perhaps on such a night it is easier to sense unseen forces abroad, and only proper to pay them homage.

But solemnity is never part of a witches' world for long, and joy returns as soon as the sacred rites are completed. Those of you familiar with the ancient folksongs of the Auvergne in southern France know their magic; the songs reflect the mysticism to be found in that region. The food of the Auvergne is magic, too, and our menu comes as welcome fare on a chilly night.

Boeuf a l'Auvergnate
5 pounds chuck beef cut in large cubes
Flour
7 tablespoons butter
6 tablespoons olive oil
Salt and freshly ground pepper
1/2 cup cognac, warmed
1/2 pound bacon, cut in dice
3 cloves garlic, chopped
3 carrots, sliced and chopped
3 medium onions, chopped
3 shallots, minced
3 tomatoes, peeled and quartered
Handful of parsley, chopped
1 bottle dry red wine
1 cup water
1/2 teaspoon dried tarragon
1 teaspoon dried thyme
1 bay leaf
1 pound mushrooms, sliced

Flour the beef cubes and brown them quickly in 4 tablespoons each of butter and olive oil in a heavy skillet. Season with salt and pepper. Pour the warmed cognac over the meat and ignite. When the flame dies, transfer the meat to a 3-quart ovenproof casserole and set aside. Preheat the oven to 350 degrees.

Sauté the bacon, garlic, carrots, onions, shallots, tomatoes and parsley in the skillet, stirring, until the bacon is lightly browned. Combine with the beef in the casserole and add the wine and enough water to just cover the ingredients. Crumble the tarragon and thyme into the liquid and add the bay leaf to bring forth flavor. Cover and bake in the moderate oven for 1 hour.

Blend a tablespoon each of butter and flour and stir into the casserole. Return the dish to the oven and continue baking for about three hours longer.

Just prior to serving, sauté the mushrooms in 2 tablespoons each of butter and olive oil until brown. Add to the casserole.

This dish may be prepared earlier in the day and reheated. Serve a green salad of romaine, watercress and endive tossed in a simple olive oil and tarragon vinegar dressing. Be sure to put out several loaves of French bread and some sweet butter. Lemon sherbet and the traditional crescent cakes are a light, right dessert.

Candlemas

By torch and taper,
Bonfire bright,
We woo the sun
On Candlemas night.

At nightfall on Candlemas Eve, February 1st, every candle and lamp in the home is lighted while bonfires blaze outdoors. The ancient theme of the holiday is to encourage the sun's swift return to northern climes and bring an end to winter. In Scandinavia, crowns of lighted candles adorn the heads of celebrants and merry choruses exhort the sun to come closer and grace the earth with its light.

A splendid way to feast at Candlemas is with a Viking *smørrebrød*, or open-faced sandwiches. The variety is boundless and just make sure to observe the rule of three different tastes to each — and no two alike. Here is fare that witches may have enjoyed feasting around the long table at the Blokula in the seventeenth century. As to combinations and decorations, give your imagination free rein. We list some possibilities to top buttered rounds of rye, pumpernickel or white bread:

Crisp bacon, tomato slice, ripe Camembert cheese
Liver paste, anchovy fillet, chopped onion
Shredded raw carrot, hard-cooked egg slice, chopped chives
Crabmeat, mustard-mayonnaise, fresh dill sprigs
Roast beef slice, tomato slice, raw onion rings
Sardines, prepared mustard, green olive slices
Chopped herring, sour cream, marinated beets
Smoked herring, watercress, finely chopped onion
Blue cheese, cucumber slice, chopped parsley
Cream cheese, tongue, sliced pickle

Glögg, Swedish hot wine punch served in mugs, is a traditional feature of Candlemas celebrations. Be sure to provide your guests with spoons to scoop up the almonds and raisins.

Glögg

1 quart dry red wine
1 quart port wine
1 cup seedless raisins
2 tablespoons grated orange peel
3 cardamon seeds, crushed
9 whole cloves
1 stick cinnamon
1 1/2 cups aquavit
1 cup sugar
1 cup blanched almonds

In a 6-quart enameled pot, mix together the wines, raisins, orange peel, cardamon seeds, cloves and cinnamon. Cover and let stand overnight.

At serving time, add the aquavit and sugar, stir and bring to a full boil over a high flame. Remove from the heat and add the almonds.

Edward Burne-Jones

BASQUE SABBAT

This rare engraving by I. Ziarnko appeared as a double-page illustration in the second edition of witch-hunter Pierre De Lancre's *Tableau de l'inconstance des mauvais anges* (A View of the Duplicity of the Messengers of Evil). The infamous book was published in Paris in 1613. De Lancre's work was an obvious attempt to justify his merciless persecution of French Basques accused of witchcraft in 1608. Despite the lurid details of the picture, the artist may have been faithfully depicting certain elements of folk revels common to the Labourd region in the seventeenth century. But there is no doubt that De Lancre distorted innocent rural festivities into a Satanic orgy.

If you look closely, you'll find letters identifying the characters and events occurring at De Lancre's version of a sabbat celebration.

A. A live goat (described by De Lancre as Satan) presides as King of the Sabbat. The animal is secured in a curious, richly decorated pulpit. In the center of the goat's crown of horns is a lighted candle from which, according to De Lancre, all the fires and candles of the sabbat are lighted.

B. The crowned Queen of the Sabbat, a comely maiden, is enthroned on the goat's right while an old woman occupies a similar seat of honor on his left. The women's royal chairs are decorated with toad-like images. Queen and Crone are attired in gowns of an earlier period and both clutch live serpents symbolizing the power to divine the future.

C. An awed child is presented to the royal trio by nude parents. The mother gestures as if to acknowledge her mate's paternity. The father, a winged Pan-like creature, attempts to direct the child's attention to the Sabbat King. De Lancre, for reasons of his own, suggests that the baby has been abducted.

D. An outlandish group partakes of the sabbat banquet. The ten diners are equally divided into naked and clothed figures. Four of the five nude demonic creatures are male and winged. The fifth, an elderly female, is portrayed without wings. Four of the five clothed diners are women wearing peasant garb; the fifth wears an ornate gown and headdress indicating nobility. De Lancre remarks that "The only meat served at the sabbat is that of carrion, hanged men, hearts of unbaptized children, and unclean animals never eaten by Christians." All that remains of the depicted feast is what appears to be the body of an infant resting on an oval platter. Notice the cat with a snake in its mouth crouching in the lower right-hand corner of the picture.

E. De Lancre's caption calls this group "poor witches, who dare not approach the high ceremonies. They are admitted only as spectators and shoved into corners." But the artist may have had more in mind. The clothed male and nude female are involved in earnest conversation. His hand is raised in negative protest as if he wants no part of the proceedings, but close behind him stand two ominous figures blocking his escape.

F. Eight dancers join hands to circle a young tree. Half of the celebrants are winged and horned creatures (one has the breasts of a female and the lower extremities of a goat). These spiritual descendants of Dionysus or Pan face outward alternating with their female companions, three nude but one fully clothed, who face the tree as they prance in a lighthearted manner. De Lancre finds the dance indecent.

G. Music for the sabbat is provided by this attractive quintet seated in the shade of an old tree. The musicians are women and

they are performing from a score on the grass before them. The pipes, harp, lute, horn and viol played with a huntsman's bow are typical instruments of the early seventeenth century.

H. This is an illustration of the back-to-back dancing so often described in witch trial records as the height of pagan lewdness. The six dancers, mature women and young girls, hold hands in a circle and face outward as they whirl to the left in traditional style. The expression on their faces suggest they are in a dreamlike state.

I. Two peasant witches concoct a strange brew in an enormous cauldron resting on a tripod. A third witch works the bel-

lows to intensify the heat of the fire fueled by skulls and bones. A lizard crouches behind her to aid her efforts. The central witch figure holds in her right hand three wriggling snakes symbolizing clairvoyance. The witch on the left holds a sickle in her left hand. Together, she and the seeress lift a toad and stare at it as if waiting for an answer.

J. Dark clouds of smoke rise from the cauldron to create visions of witches on broomsticks, winged demons and dragons. One emaciated old woman rides a sea monster as she holds aloft the symbol of the diviner.

K. An elderly witch accompanied by two children arrives at the sabbat riding a goat. They seem to have emerged from the billowing smoke of the caudron. De Lancre fails to mention the shadowy form of a woman in a dark cavern below the trio. She is partially clothed in a shroud and recoils in terror at the sight of the scene before her.

L. De Lancre identifies this elegant group as "Great Lords and Ladies, and other rich and powerful witches who conduct the important business of the sabbat, where they often appear disguised or masked, so that they will not be recognized."

M. Five unmindful youngsters amuse themselves by holding at bay with long sticks a multitude of toads in a tiny pool.

The difcouerie

of witchcraft,

Wherein the lewde dealing of witches
and witchmongers is notablie detected, the
knauerie of coniurors, the impietie of inchan-
tors, the follie of foothfaiers, the impudent falf-
hood of coufenors, the infidelitie of atheifts,
the peftilent practifes of Pythonifts, the
curiofitie of figurecafters, the va-
nitie of dreamers, the begger-
lie art of Alcu-
myftrie,

The abhomination of idolatrie, the hor-
rible art of poifoning, the vertue and power of
naturall magike, and all the conueiances
of Legierdemaine and iuggling are deciphered :
and many other things opened, which
haue long lien hidden, howbeit
verie neceffarie to
be knowne.

Heerevnto is added a treatife vpon the
nature and fubftance of fpirits and diuels,
&c : all latelie written
by Reginald Scot.
Efquire.
1. Iohn.4, 1.
Beleeue not euerie fpirit, but trie the fpirits, whether they are
of God ; for manie falfe prophets are gone
out into the world, &c.
1584

Title page from the first edition of Reginald Scot's *The Discoverie of Witchcraft.* London (1584)

10   BOOKS AND MEMORIES

Gothic Tales

Insight into the nature of the unseen world often comes from unlikely sources. Writers of gothic and macabre tales, for instance, can create a feeling of the power of the transcendent almost in spite of themselves.

H. P. Lovecraft offers a prime example of this ability. A horror-story writer during the nineteen twenties and thirties, Lovecraft is preserved for our time through the advocacy of the late August Derleth and his publishing firm, Arkham House. *The Dunwich Horror and Other Stories* contains an excellent introduction to Lovecraft's work by Derleth. *The Tomb and Other Tales* is also an indispensable work of the Lovecraft canon.

Lovecraft, of course, followed a tradition in which reality was unimportant. His goal was to fascinate and terrify readers and leave us with a shivery fear of dark corners and old places. Toward this end Lovecraft invented a pantheon of primal incorporeal entities, with names such as Azathoth and Hastur, who wait malevolently for a chance to visit horror on the world.

Such work may be viewed as harmful to some, for it fosters fear and hostility toward forces many of us believe are neither good nor evil but are simply there. Yet

the power with which Lovecraft invokes a realm of existence beyond the one we see and touch testifies to its presence. Reading him, we experience a source of knowledge beyond the senses. We don't learn about this realm but recognize it, even though it is grossly distorted. Any sensitive reader of *The Dunwich Horror* or *The Haunter of the Dark*, for example, will experience this insight, though we must disregard the implacable enmity toward our world with which Lovecraft endows his beings.

Through the ages storytellers and writers have used their fancies to entertain us. Skillful ones such as H.P. Lovecraft plumbed their souls to strike universal chords that resonate in people attuned to such unheard sounds. Adept readers can divine much about these chords through the work of such imaginative writers.

— CHARLES E. PEPPER

Fairy Tales

Until recently the world of children's books was controlled by conscientious editors mainly concerned with building reading skills and instilling what they considered correct social attitudes. Their commendable goals often resulted in dull books destined to discourage reading at an early age. What of nourishment for the spirit? What of the wild, bizarre enchantment of old-time fairy tales and folk tales? Myths and legends handed down from one

generation to the next, long before the advent of the printed word, are precious. Enriching childhood, they form the notion of good rewarded and evil punished. Those spirited stories awaken imagination and quicken the young mind to see beyond mere appearance to true value. In a guileless way, they serve their purpose and delight young readers.

For the student of witchcraft the ancient tales provide an excellent source of information. Although her name was changed to fairy godmother, the bestower of gifts was in fact the wise woman of the village — the witch. Here she is in an old illustration: pointed hat, wand and the power to make Cinderella's dream come true.

Arthur Rackham

Margaret Evans Price

Briar Rose, or Sleeping Beauty, reveals the age-old custom of wishing a special gift upon a child.

Once upon a time a King and Queen gave a christening feast for a long-awaited child. To the celebration the royal couple invited seven fairies (or witches) of the kingdom in the hope they would bestow upon the infant princess special gifts as was their custom.

Unfortunately they neglected to invite one rather bad-tempered fairy. Angered by the slight, she arrived at the feast in a rage. As the fairies began to give their gifts, the wisest of the seven waited, hidden behind the cradle, for she feared the wrath of the angry one.

Beauty was the present bestowed by the youngest fairy; wit was granted by the next; the third offered grace;

the fourth, virtue; the fifth, a lovely voice; the sixth, a smile to win all hearts. Then the bad-tempered fairy stepped forward and pointing her ivory wand like a spear at the royal baby, she cried out: "While still in her rose-bud youth the King's daughter shall prick her hand with a spindle and fall down dead."

Hearing this the company despaired, but the wise fairy said: "Although I cannot undo what has been done, it will not be quite as she commanded. Your daughter will prick her hand with a spindle and fall to the floor, but she will not die. Instead her sleep will last for one hundred years and from that sleep, when her dream is over, a king's son shall awaken her."

Here is the inevitability of a Greek tragedy, yet the promise of a happy ending, in witchcraft, you see, hope is believed to be the most singular of human attributes.

And then the world of children's books changed! Rave reviews and major awards greeted author J.K. Rowling upon publication of her first novel, *Harry Potter and the Sorcerer's Stone*. Wonder of wonders, the book became an international phenomenon. The book intended for young readers crossed over to delight an adult audience as well. A new century dawned and a new attitude toward witchcraft arrived as Harry Potter becomes a classic literary figure.

The Grimoires

Medieval texts of ritual magic in manuscript form are preserved in the British Museum, the Bibliotheque Nationale and the Bibliotheque d'Arsenal in Paris, the libraries of the Vatican in Rome, and in private collections. A few grimoires have been printed. Excerpts from others appeared in books about ceremonial magic published over the last three centuries. These are the most famous of the conjuring books:

The Clavicle (Key) of Solomon.
The Lemegeton (Lesser Key) of Solomon
Testament of Solomon
The Secrets of the Great Albert (Le Grand Albert)
The Secrets of Little Albert (Le Petit Albert)
The Grimoire of Pope Honorius
Constitution of Honorius
The Great Grimoire
The Grimorium Verum (True)
The Heptameron (Magical Elements) Peter of Abano
The Enchiridion
The Red Dragon
The Black Hen

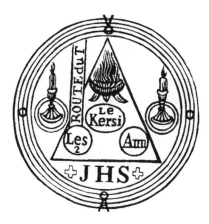

Historical Witchcraft

Several excellent general histories of witchcraft are available. Any one of the following books serve well as an introduction to the subject:

Witchcraft, Charles Williams
Four Centuries of Witch Beliefs, R.T. Davies
Witchcraft, Pennethorne Hughes

In 1921 Dr. Margaret A. Murray, the Egyptologist and anthropologist, presented her theory of witchcraft as a survival of a pre-Christian religious cult. Her books set off a controversy that continues to the present day.

The Witch-Cult in Western Europe
The God of the Witches
The Divine King in England

Dr. Murray was regarded by academics as an authority on witchcraft until a majority of scholars decided that her conclusions were reckless.

Montague Summers was another controversial historian of witchcraft. Credulity is the word most often used to describe his works, for Summers was firmly convinced that witchcraft was evil and inspired by Satan:

The History of Witchcraft and Demonology
The Geography of Witchcraft
Witchcraft and Black Magic

Scores of scholarly studies of witchcraft are as marred by their skepticism as Summers' books are by his insistence that witches are agents of evil.

Witch Hunting and Witch Trials, C. L'Estrange Ewen
The World of Witches, Julio C. Baroja
The European Witch-Craze of the 16th and 17th Centuries, H.R. Trevor-Roper
Religion & the Decline of Magic, Keith Thomas

But the pendulum begins to swing in another direction. Two books in recent years presented refreshing and novel viewpoints of the subject of witchcraft.

Witches: Investigating an Ancient Religion, T.C. Lethbridge
The Roots of Witchcraft, Michael Harrison

Modern Witchcraft

Sir James G. Frazer's *The Golden Bough*, Jane Harrison's *Prolegomena*, *The White Goddess* by Robert Graves, the books of folklorist Charles G. Leland, the works of Margaret Murray and the research of Jung have all been instrumental in the rise of neo-witchcraft. Two other major figures of the twentieth century who served to revitalize interest in the occult are Aleister Crowley and Gerald Gardner.

Crowley was a ceremonial magician of rare talent and unusual ability. His books are receiving unprecedented attention today after years of neglect. Occult booksellers list over twenty volumes devoted to Crowley's thought:

Gerald Gardner's books, some long out of print, have been reissued.

High Magic's Aid
Witchcraft Today
The Meaning of Witchcraft

Many books about magic include chapters on witchcraft. Three excellent studies:

The Black Arts, Richard Cavendish
Ritual Magic, Francis King
The Occult, Colin Wilson

Many authors present witchcraft in a favorable light. Most are highly personal accounts and all are eminently readable.

Witchcraft, the Sixth Sense, Justine Glass
Mastering Witchcraft, Paul Huson
The Complete Art of Witchcraft, Sybil Leek
Natural Magic, Doreen Valiente

Positive Magic, Marion Weinstein
The Spiral Dance, Starhawk (Miriam Simos)
Hedge Witch, Rae Beth

Glimpses of Aleister Crowley

So much has been written about Aleister Crowley, mostly denunciatory, that he has become something of an occult legend. Two descriptions follow by writers who knew him. The first is taken from W. Somerset Maugham's introduction to the reissue of his novel *The Magician*, in which Crowley is the protagonist. Aleister Crowley spent the winter of 1907 in Paris, as did Maugham.

"I took an immediate dislike to him, but he interested and amused me. He was a great talker and he talked uncommonly well. In early youth, I was told, he was extremely handsome, but when I knew him he had put on weight, and his hair was thinning. He had fine eyes and a way, whether natural or acquired I do not know, of focusing them that, when he looked at you, he seemed to look behind you. He was a fake, but not entirely a fake. At Cambridge he had won his chess blue and was esteemed the best whist player of his time. He was a liar and unbecomingly boastful, but the odd thing was that he had actually done some of the things he boasted of. As a mountaineer, he had made an ascent of K.2 in the Hindu Kush, the second highest mountain in India, and he made it without elaborate equipment, the cylinders of oxygen and so forth, which render endeavors of the mountaineers of the present day more likely to succeed. He did not reach the top, but got nearer to it than anyone had done before.

"At the time I knew him he was dabbling in Satanism, magic and the occult. There was just then something of a vogue in Paris for that sort of thing, occasioned, I surmised, by the interest that was still taken in a book by Huysmans, *La Bas*. Crowley told fantastic stories of his experiences, but it was hard to say whether he was telling the truth or merely pulling your leg. During that winter I saw him several times, but never after I left Paris to return to London."

William Seabrook, in his delightful book *Witchcraft, Its Power in the World Today*, remembers his first meeting with Crowley.

"It was through the late Frank Harris that I first met Aleister Crowley, around 1917, in New York. Crowley was living in No.1 University Place, to the utter terror of two conventional ladies from the South who had rented him the ground floor. He was a Cambridge man, a distinguished poet, was in many British anthologies, including

the *Oxford Book of English Mystical Verse*. He had been in the Himalayas as a mountain climber, was supposed to have studied Tibetan lore. I was wanting to meet Crowley because he was supposed to be an authority on medieval sorcery, and was pleased when Frank Harris arranged it.

"We met at lunch in Mouquin's. Aleister Crowley was a strange, disturbing fellow, with a heavy pontifical manner mixed with a good deal of sly, monkeylike, and occasionally malicious humor. He wore an enormous star sapphire on the forefinger of his right hand, and later sprouted an American Indian warlock which curled slightly and made him resemble (with his round, smooth-shaven face and big, round eyes) a nursery imp masquer-ading as Mephistopheles. The talk at that luncheon left me gasping. Frank Harris was one of the greatest conversationlists of this or any other century, and Crowley talked like Pain's Fireworks." Seabrook continues with several pages of reminiscences, too long to quote here but well worth reading, and concludes:

"I am possibly too casual, but feel that the British in general have been a bit too heavy in their attitude toward Crowley. If he had been an American, I can't help feeling that we'd have had more fun with him. As a matter of fact we did, while he was over here. I saw him last in Paris in 1933. We lunched, on his invitation, at Foyot's. He was still having a good deal of fun with the world."

A Tribute to Gerald Gardner

In England, the last law against witchcraft was repealed in 1951. The repeal was of immense importance. It meant that after centuries of hiding, witches could once again openly practice their faith. Yet they had learned to be cautious; the witches remained hidden.

At that time Gerald Gardner, an ardent occultist, belonged to a coven that he felt was possibly one of the last. Before that too disappeared, Gardner wanted to provide a misinformed and often hostile public with realistic information about the practice of witchcraft. He wished to write with exactitude about what witches did, what witches believed.

Gardner had been born into a well-to-do family of Scottish ancestry. At an early age he was influenced by the works of the spiritualist Florence Marryat, and from this source Gardner developed a firm belief in the survival of the spirit after death. He spent much of his life roaming the globe, and from his time spent in the East, Gardner accepted the idea of many gods and spirits.

The young occultist got his first job at the age of sixteen, working on a tea plantation in Ceylon. Gardner spent much time in the jungle associating with tribespeople and learning of their beliefs and magical practices. In 1908 he moved on to Borneo, among the headhunting Dyaks, and from there roved to Malaya. From plantation work, Gardner went into government employ — in 1923 as inspector of rubber plantations and later as a customs officer. Wherever he went, whatever his job, Gardner never ceased to observe tribal customs and magical practice. He studied anthropology and worked at archaeology. Gardner's first major book, *Kris and Other Malay Weapons*, became the standard work on the subject and established him as a world authority. He became equally distinguished for his archaeological excavations. Gardner's discovery of the ancient city of Singapura won him an honorary doctorate from Singapore University. Both the Singapore Museum and the Victoria and Albert Museum in London house his reconstructions of ancient seagoing ships.

It was not until Gardner's retirement and return to England, however, that he came in contact with witchcraft. He discovered the existence of a coven in the New Forest, and after a waiting period became an initiate. Gardner's interest as an anthropologist/folklorist was stimulated, and he was extremely happy and excited by his initiation. His joy was caused by learning that witchcraft was still alive, and that it was not Satanism and anti-Christian mumbo jumbo, but a belief system dating from pre-Christian times. Gardner's first impulse was to rush out and tell the world it was badly informed about witchcraft. He was not allowed to do so by his coven.

Gardner continued to travel. He was able, through his experiences and learning, to find many parallels with witchcraft in other societies and civilizations. Gardner came to recognize the origin of many practices within the craft that witches accepted without question. He believed he'd found instances in which, over centuries of secret practice errors had crept into the rituals. And he set about to correct them.

In 1949 Gardner was rather grudgingly permitted publication of his book, *High Magic's Aid*. The book was written entertainingly as a novel, but gave a truer picture of witchcraft than any other popular book up to that time.

Dr. Margaret Murray had theorized in 1921 that witchcraft was an ancient religion having no connection with Christianity. It was not until 1954, however, that Gardner's next book seemed to confirm her theory. In that year Gardner was finally allowed by his coven to publish a factual book for the general public. Following publica-

tion of *Witchcraft Today*, Gardner was surprised and delighted to receive letters from covens throughout Western Europe. Each coven had thought that perhaps its particular witches were the last survivors, and each coven was wonderfully happy to hear of Gerald Gardner's group.

In addition to his books, Gardner further provided the public with information by opening the first museum of magic and witchcraft. The musuem in Castletown, Isle of Man, housed his fantastic collection of religio-magical artifacts from around the world. By this time Gardner had long since achieved the degree of High Priest within his coven and was now very much regarded (unofficially, of course) as the Grand Old Man of witchcraft.

Yet things were far from easy and Gerald Gardner paid a high price for his truthfulness. What Gardner did took a great deal of courage, and also cost him money. To claim to be a witch in those days was to invite people to throw rocks through your windows, to be slandered, to be ridiculed. Yet all this Gardner endured, for he felt that someone had to give the true picture of witchcraft and no

one else was willing to do so. Today's witches — even the "commercial" ones — owe Gardner a great debt.

The coven which Gardner originally joined was a Celtic group; as in Christianity there are various denominations, so in witchcraft. In later years Gardner reviewed the fragmented rituals preserved by his coven and brought them back to what he believed were their original forms. Followers of these rituals came to be known as "Gardnerian" witches. Since the name does honor to Gerald Gardner's work, it is a good one.

In the winter of 1964, as Gardner was returning to England from Lebanon, he died at sea. His body was taken ashore and buried at Tunis the following day — February 13th. On that day witchcraft lost a great exponent.

— RAYMOND BUCKLAND

Departure for the sabbat   Engraved from a painting by David Teniers, 17th century

11 MYSTICAL TECHNIQUES

Revery

To perform an act of magic one must have complete utilization of the senses, the mind and the will. Attaining full mastery of these faculties requires study and discipline. Those with inherent gifts often unknowingly train themselves. Others who may be only faintly aware of latent talent can, through rigorous work, develop their powers to an astonishing degree. All can benefit from the exercises outlined here.

Every human is endowed with a degree of imagination and visual recall. In the practice of witchcraft, it is essential that these qualities be sharpened to a fine point. You must, upon command, be able to summon up a place, an atmosphere, a face so vividly that you can almost reach out and touch it. Consider for a moment how well your subconscious mind performs this feat in dreams. You can train your conscious mind to do just as well.

Perhaps a word of warning is in order. Once you begin to explore your psychic perception, you have entered a path of no return. It is likely that you will never think or feel in quite the same way again. Usually the reward outweighs the danger, but you should consider the matter carefully before proceeding. An adept whose name is forgotten, though his words are not, said, "By the time power is attained, judgement has matured enough to use it wisely." So mote it be!

PREPARATION

We are night people and in all likelihood so are you. When the sun goes down we feel more alive, happier and keener. For this reason and because it usually offers fewer distractions for the senses, night is the best time to practice these exercises. Complete all tasks that merit attention before nightfall lest they divert you. Assure yourself of an hour or two of quiet privacy. Dress comfortably in loose garments and keep the feet bare.

SENSUAL EXTENSIONS
(as preface to each exercise)

Set out stimulants for each of the five senses. These should be of your own preferences, but as suggestions:

SCENT — *pine incense*
TOUCH — *glass vase*
FLAVOR — *dry red wine*
SOUND — *hand bell*
SIGHT— *color swatch*

Thoughtfully extend each sense in turn by shutting off the others. The odor of the lighted incense will fill your being. The touch experience should encompass the kinesthetic sense of your own movement as well as an appreciation of the actual surface you touch. The flavor extension is sharper if you choose a stimulant unfamiliar to your taste. As you listen to the reverberations of the bell, concentrate on them alone. A length of fabric in a color particularly appealing to you is the best choice at this stage of visual extension. Later on, an abstract painting or a Tarot card may be used.

You will come to know how much time to devote to each sensation. When all the senses are satisfied, stand motionless for as long as you comfortably can. This exercises the hidden sense of balance.

ENTERING THE NETHER WORLD

Recline or sit, as you choose. Drop all tensions and shut off the senses you have just extended, one by one, in this order: smell not…feel not…taste not…hear not…see not. Try to imagine yourself in a world without sensation. Surrender to it and float in nothingness. You are now in what we call the nether world—or, if you prefer, a trance state. To sustain thoughtless suspension is difficult, but becomes easier with practice.

COLOR RECALL

Now fill the empty world with a color. Let it surround you. Bathe in its light. Recall all the things you know that possess this color and will their images to appear before

you. Should the color be green, call up the foliage of spring and grassy fields. Wander back to childhood, when impressions were more vivid. Climb a tree, roll in the grass.

An error often made in an initial attempt at color recall is to think in terms of a screen or flat surface. Understandable, of course, we live in a world of film and television viewing. But the key to success is to participate in the sensation — to immerse in it, not view it.

This is usually enough for a first lesson. Practice as often as possible until you can summon color when you wish.

IMMEDIATE IMPRESSION RECALL

Perform the preliminary sensual extensions and hold the period of motionlessness for as long as you can. Before entering the nether world, light a candle in your darkened room. Concentrate on whatever falls into your line of vision. Study the scene intently. Now close your eyes and see it again. Question yourself to separate what your mind knows from what your inner eye sees. Should you fail, try again with half-closed eyes to record the impression. It may take quite a while before the image will swim up before your inner eye, but you can be sure that it will.

Supplement this exercise with
INTERVAL RECALL

On the following day, during "lost time," on a bus or waiting for someone, attempt to see again the image you sought the previous night. Even a fleeting glimpse is worthwhile. Continue to pursue interval recall throughout the day whenever an opportunity presents itself. Try to think of your study as an ongoing event, without beginning or end.

EMOTIONAL RECALL

Enter the nether world and let your mind relive a happy or a bitter experience. Pay close attention to the details of the memory — time of year, sound, color, the whole feeling of the scene. Know again your joy, misery, embarrassment or pain. Sense your pulse rate quicken, your face flush, your tension mount. To recapture the moment more accurately, you might use sensual stimulants that apply to the experience — perfume or shaving lotion. Play a melody you associate with the time. The memory is usually less poignant in recall, but there will be moments when the recollection will flood back with its initial impact. But now you are using the experience as an exercise, and you will feel refreshed rather than drained by its force.

TESTING YOUR PROGRESS

Have you mastered the art of Revery to the extent that you can successfully exchange an image or a thought with another person? Choose a friend with whom you enjoy unusual rapport — preferably one who has embarked on the same course of study. The experiments may be carried out in the same room or miles apart. Set up a time for the receiver to enter the nether world while the sender forcefully projects a series of three images. It is wise for the receiver to have pencil and paper at hand in order to record whatever comes through. You may establish a category. Color is a good choice for initial transmissions. But it is important that the receiver make note of all impressions that come through, however unusual or unexpected. The notes may prove enlightening upon later examination. Be sure to trade roles, for a gifted sender may not be an able receiver.

Adepts through the ages have suggested means to aid you in your quest. Baths, fasting or induced fatigue have been advised. Progress can be infuriatingly slow — periods of swift advance and times of dismal failure. Any endeavor requiring discipline knows this is a typical process. The comfort is that every human possesses the potential for success. The attainment can be a pleasure for everyone, but for the witch it is vital.

Love's Secret

Never seek to tell thy love,
Love that never told can be:
For the gentle wind doth move
Silently, invisibly.
— WILLIAM BLAKE

Love and magic are akin. Both arts may be learned but not taught. Neither rely on reason, nor can their power or beauty be readily explained.

Eliphas Levi, the renowned ceremonial magician, listed the rules of the Magus: To Know, To Dare, To Will, To Keep Silence. Silence is particularly relevant in love: a tenet of witchcraft holds the act of love to be sacred and warns that communication between lovers is often confused by words. "Speak not lest ye break the spell." Other sources echo the same theme. Jalalud-din Rumi, a Persian poet of the thirteenth century, commented, "Explanation by the tongue makes most things clear. But love unexplained is better."

When you find true love (do not settle for less), accord it the awe and respect the emotion deserves. Do not question it or demand in tiresome words the worthless vows so often broken. Love is magic and will live without definition — like the gentle wind, silently, invisibly.

Aubrey Beardsley

Image Magic

Image magic is universal. Evidence of the use of this particular charm occurs from prehistoric time to the present day on every continent and in every culture. Although often practiced with malevolence, it also has beneficial aspects. Frequently employed in the healing arts or for the protection of a loved one engaged in a dangerous pursuit, this form of sympathetic magic may be used as a love charm too—either to regain lost love or to attract a desirable stranger.

In its most usual form, a likeness of the recipient of good will or the intended victim is fashioned from clay or wax. The addition to the substance of a personal possession or an individual attribute is said to increase chances of success. The effigy, with proper ceremony, may be anointed with healing oils, encircled with sacred herbs or passed through the smoke of incense. If prepared with evil intent, it might be pierced with pins, broken in pieces, or if of wax, melted slowly in fire. The function of the puppet, of course, is to provide the sorcerer with a focal point for intense concentration. Results depend entirely upon the strength of will the practitioner can summon.

Dance

That dance can be more than just good exercise or the sheer pleasure derived from rhythmic movement is obvious to those who study the art of magic. Hardly a phase of occult history is without a reference to the use of dance as a means of entry into a mystical state for the purpose of worship, divination or the gathering of power from the atmosphere itself. Initiates to the Eleusinian and Dionysian Mysteries of ancient Greece, members of the witch cult in Western Europe, the Sufi dervishes and the practitioners of Voodoo or Obeah in the West Indies all provide instances of the efficacy of dance as a key to hidden knowledge.

A most vivid description regarding the exhilaration of mystic dance is found in Dion Fortune's *Psychic Self-Defense*:

"Then I went away for my summer holiday and found myself on the summit of a high and isolated hill on a day of bright sun and high wind. I was very conscious of the nearness of the elemental kingdoms. The air seemed full of silver sparkles, which is always a sign that the veil is thin. There was no one present save some friends who were sympathetic. I faced into the wind and raised my arms in invocation. Then all of us, without any suggestion of leadership, began the Dance of the Elements, whirling like dancing dervishes upon that hilltop. Fortunately nobody was about, but I don't know that it would have made much difference if they had been, for we were caught up out of ourselves and the air seemed full of rushing golden flames, lying level in the wind. For days afterwards we seemed charged with elemental energy by that extraordinary dance."

How reminiscent this twentieth-century account is of the whirling ecstasy of the medieval sabbat celebrations. That divination too might have enriched the sabbat experience is suggested by this translation of a curious inscription found in a thirteenth-century chateau in southern France.

> *The twelve dance on high —*
> *Who dances not, knoweth not*
> *What comes to pass.*

With gifts such as these it is no wonder that the church fathers forbade dancing and associated its joys with evil.

In order that a circle dance can achieve its mystic purpose, an inner harmony should exist between performing couples. To explore the subjective affinities of partners and discover couples attuned to one another, an exercise borrowed from theater dance classes has proven effective in modern witchcraft. A leader is chosen. Setting: A large empty room with a high ceiling, dark save for lighted candles held by each one of the assembled group.

Music: Dramatic, with a strong beat.

Action: Upon a signal from the leader, an even number of the participants walk at random around the room, sensing the music and loosening the muscles of the body. When the time is judged right, all join hands to form a circle. Tension is established by stretching the arms sideways to bring the circle to its full diameter. Dropping hands, all retreat nine steps, taking care to keep the circle intact. A facing couple is then directed to move toward one another and meet in the center. When they are face to face, an inner response provokes an action. They may circle each

other, even abruptly turn away, or they may begin to improvise a dance. The prelude, meeting and return to original position should be instinctive — each person surrendering to the moment, heedless of the onlookers. The exercise continues until every combination of partners has been tested. It should be immediately apparent to the observing leader which pairs are most likely to perform in harmony and add a vital element to sacred dance.

Tools

They say the tools of a witch are found. Power attends the implements discovered in a dusty attic, old barn, antique shop, or perhaps among the effects of a departed relative. By instinct you will recognize your own, and chances are strong that the object you find will seem familiar to your eyes and to your hand.

The ceremonial magician declares that tools must be new and never used before for any purpose. Witchcraft requires only that they be marked and dedicated to your use. The mark must be one you associate with yourself — an initial, a rune, a personal design. The consecration is simple but essential. Grasp the article firmly in your hand and chant aloud:

Now the powers of darkness rise,
To hear my wish and then fulfill,
The tool I hold as servant be
Unto my hand, my heart, my will

It is not customary for a witch to keep tools hidden away. The cauldron may be near the hearth innocently holding magazines or newspapers as if that is its function. A goblet or bell may rest upon a shelf. As many have learned, the best hiding place is often in plain sight. The magician or adept, on the other hand, guards tools with great care; they are often wrapped in linen or parchment and locked away. The difference reflects contrary attitudes regarding magic — the ceremonial magician seeks to dominate the supernatural while the witch only knows and respects it.

The following list includes tools of both wizard and witch.

The Wand or *Staff* should be of wood — hazel, willow, beech are popular choices. Ivory or ebony were favored in the past and rarely found today.

The Bell can reflect personal taste in design, but sound is the important factor. It should reverberate pleasantly to the ear.

The Cauldron must be of cast iron and have three legs.

A Goblet or *Chalice* may be as simple as this ancient Gothic design. It should be of silver.

Sun and *Moon Symbols* can range from witch balls to graphic representations.

A Brazier is used in lieu of a fireplace and holds burning coals.

Boxes are essential items needed to hold feathers, shells, pebbles or gems. No occult household is without a great assortment of boxes.

An Incense Burner can be a simple wooden holder or perhaps one of ornamental brass.

Candle Holders may be of any material — wood, bronze, silver or wrought iron. We picture one in brass of Romanesque style. The lovely designs of colonial America are chosen by many in the craft.

The Ritual Knife or *Athame* as described in magical texts has a black handle and is symbolically inscribed on the blade.

Further equipment might include parchment paper and india ink, skeins of woolen yarn in red, black, white and green, dried herbs and roots, blessed oils and water and a book of shadows, inherited, found, or of your own devising.

The Still Point

A striking description of what witches call the still point occurs in the last act of Eugene O'Neill's haunting play, *Long Day's Journey into Night*, when Edmund recalls a time at sea:

"I lay on the bowsprit, facing astern, with the water foaming into spume under me, the masts with every sail white in the moonlight, towering high above me. I became drunk with the beauty and singing rhythm of it, and for a moment I lost myself — actually lost my life. I was set free! I dissolved in the sea, became white sails and flying spray, became beauty and rhythm, became moonlight and the ship and the high dim-starred sky! I belonged, without past or future, within peace and unity and a wild joy, within something greater than my own life, or the life of Man, to Life itself!"

Awareness of another reality may come unbidden. Certain circumstances can accidently provoke a mystical experience, for transcendence is not the exclusive property of Eastern holy men or medieval Christian saints. It belongs to all humans, and the Greeks knew it.

Ecstatic union, our still point, was possibly experienced by initiates into the Greek Mysteries. Very little is known about them, but it was said that through symbolic ritual the inner eye was opened and the power of perception increased to the extent that a higher degree of reality was realized. Initiation was not restricted on grounds of race, sex, age or class. One reason for exclusion does appear in a cryptic statement by Plato, "He who not being inspired, and having no touch of madness in his soul, comes to the door and thinks he will get into the temple by the help of art — he, I say, and his poetry are not admitted." But during the centuries while the Mysteries flourished many ordinary people had the necessary "touch of madness" and were endowed by initiation with what Jung termed "a remarkable instance of exaltation."

From the sixth century B.C. on we find recorded accounts of that formless intuition, a mystical union with "the One." Plotinus, a Neo-Platonist philosopher of the third century A.D., called the illumination "a flight of the alone to the Alone" and observed that "The vision is for him who will see it and he who has seen it knows what I say." Jacob Boehme, William Blake, Aleister Crowley as well as long-distance runners and mountain climbers have all found the other reality. The means of attainment are myriad: asceticism, sexual abandon, fasting, dance, exhaustion, prayer, exercise, breath control, drugs, delirium and self-hypnosis have all been used with success.

The solitary witch seeks the still point through self-hypnosis, for it is the most natural method and the easiest to control. To master the will requires patience and long practice, but "once achieved, never lost" is a comforting fact. But even with a strong, well-trained will, reaching the still point is rare. Yet it is probable that anyone who seeks higher reality will find it at least once during the course of a lifetime. Should it elude you, the discipline exercised bestows other gifts. It is as if visual fixation somehow centers the being. It not only promotes mental health, but gives peace and strength to the spirit.

Seeking the Still Point

For one hour of each day within the time of the waning moon, alone and in the proper mood and setting, concentrate your eyes on a forechosen bright object: a candle flame, crystal ball or similar shining surface. The mystic Jacob Boehme "gazed fixidly upon a burnished pewter dish which reflected the sunshine with great brilliance." Never waver your glance, and from deep within you summon the whole strength of your will to bear upon it. The length of intense concentration will steadily increase with practice.

Light a Candle

Tonight in total darkness, light a candle. To fully appreciate the experience and honor the act in a proper way, recite an old chant:

> *Spirit of fury, spirit of flame,*
> *I smite the darkness with thy name.*

Murmur the name of any one of the fire deities — Vesta, Vulcan, Loki — as you strike a match and in one action, touch the flame to the candlewick.

Study the flame now as it sways to reveal your own breath and the air currents in the room. It is easy to understand why the element of fire was so venerated by the ancients. You may feel a quiet contentment as you gaze steadily at the bright light before you.

Candles were used in religious rites as early as 3000 B.C. And they retained their sacred nature, for it was not until the Middle Ages that the wax candle came into general use as a means of illumination in the household.

In witchcraft and ceremonial magic, lighting a candle is a usual prelude to sorcery. The practical reason underlying the rite is the need to concentrate psychic energy; the flame serves as a focal point. Beeswax candles formed by your own hand in any color you feel appropriate is the rule of witches. The ceremonial magician, however, follows a stricter path. The candles must be made by the practitioner from virgin wax (that taken from bees having made it for the first time), according to *The Key of Solo-*

mon. The color of the wax is of vital importance and must correspond to the planet under whose rule the ritual will be performed.

Sun — gold or yellow
Moon — silver or white
Mars — red
Mercury — mixed or purple
Jupiter — blue
Venus — green
Saturn — black

Some occult traditions require that the candle be anointed with oil, wrapped in parchment and buried in the earth (wick pointing north) for the interval of a moon's phase prior to the rite.

It is fortunate that beeswax candles not only burn best but are the easiest to make. Requirements are simple: a room at an eighty-degree temperature, a sharp knife and a smooth board on which to roll and cut the wax. Round wicks and the solid or honeycomb sheets of colored beeswax are easily available from craft supply houses.

Many candle spells exist. Old English folklore provides a way to summon a lover. Thrust two common pins through a lighted candle's wick to form an "X" and softly say:

It's not this candle alone I stick,
But my lover's heart I mean to prick.
Whether asleep or awaken be,
I charge his (or her) spirit to come to me.

When the flame has burned down to the crossed pins, the desired lover will either appear in a dream or in person within a fortnight.

Defense Against Psychic Attack

Psychic forces can be generated by intense emotion. Hatred channeled by the power of a strong, well-trained will is a dangerous weapon. And revenge when clearly visualized with firm intent is liable to become a hostile reality.

At the outset of a psychic attack the victim often experiences an odd feeling of futility. Dejected spirits may lead to unreasonable panic and if pressure mounts, health is in jeopardy. It becomes increasingly difficult to think or act rationally and many surrender without a battle. Steps may be taken to deflect a psychic assault before it has time to develop.

The first rule of defense is to relax the body. Match the siege with the cunning of nature. If you have ever had occasion to restrain an animal you know how it will seem

to go limp in your grasp. The intent is to judge the captor's concentration. The moment your attention wavers, the creature will struggle free. In similar fashion, a tree or plant will bend with the wind rather than defy it.

Try to determine the identity of your enemy. An amateur, even one enraged, seldom has the fortitude to do serious damage. Take a purifying bath with a drop or two of a pleasant essential oil and afterwards, create a circle of fire (holding a lighted candle, face the east and turn in place three times). This is often enough to deal with the problem.

However, if your attacker is an adept in magic, a more elaborate strategy is required. Begin with the bath, follow with an anointing of oil on forehead, shoulders and breast in the sign of the pentagram while chanting:

In the name of mercy,
With the power of fate,
Pray attend me now
While my need is great.

Lay out a protective barrier; a circle formed by objects you especially cherish — clothes to bric-a-brac — all should hold special significance for you and have been touched often by you. Sit on the floor in the middle of the circle with your knees drawn up to your chin. Grasp your legs with both arms and lightly rest your head on your knees. Close your eyes and repeat aloud any rhyme or lyric of a song you know by heart until the words lose their meaning to monotony. Remain in an attitude of contemplation until you no longer feel threatened.

Maintain protection with sacred herbs and sea water. Wear an amulet or talisman as a safeguard. Some choose to answer their attacker in kind but as this requires a great emotional investment, the game is seldom worth the candle.

Only that which does not teach, which does not cry out,
which does not condescend, which does not explain, is irresistible.

— W. B. YEATS

Afterword

Manhattan's Greenwich Village has always attracted adventurous young people from all over the world, and the atmosphere was especially electric following World War II. At that time John Wilcock, an English journalist from Yorkshire, met Elizabeth Pepper, a writer/artist from New England. Since one witch knows another on sight, we formed a friendship that was to change our lives. Together we set about to create a journal dedicated to the beauty, deep wisdom and simple good sense present in the craft. In 1971 this dream became a reality when Grosset & Dunlap published the first *Witches' Almanac*. Its immediate success surprised the publishing world, for at the time the effort was considered an anomaly—too far removed from the mainstream.

Perhaps the most remarkable response to *The Witches' Almanac* has been the enthusiasm it evokes from readers. From the first edition to the current issue, an astonishing number of letters have expressed appreciation. It is almost as if we have managed to touch a lost chord and satisfy a hidden need within the human spirit, and it is a joy to continue compiling our annual compendium of the craft.

The Witches' Almanac readers are wonderfully diverse: male and female, rich and poor, rural and urban, aged nine to eighty-four — you would dismay a demographer with your variety. And it is the sympathy and awareness in your correspondence that links all this diversity — a concern for nature and our animal kin, humor and warmth, a sense of wonder and a lively taste for life's mystery and magic hover over our mailbox. We read with pleasure every letter that comes in and wish we could answer in kind. The numbers are too overwhelming. But we feel very fortunate indeed to be in touch with so many kindred souls inspiring our continuing efforts.